THE MANOR HOUSES OF ENGLAND

Grimshaw Hall, Warwickshire.

THE MANOR HOUSES OF ENGLAND

By
P. H. Ditchfield M.A., F.S.A.
Illustrated by
Sydney R. Jones

Bracken Books
LONDON

This edition published 1985 by Bracken Books,
a division of Bestseller Publications Ltd,
Brent House, 24 Friern Park, North Finchley, London N12.
under licence from the proprietor.

ISBN 0 946495 26 2

Printed and bound by R. J. Acford, Chichester, England.

PREFACE

THE object of this book is to describe and illustrate the old country manor-houses of England, which are fast falling into decay, and are being replaced by modern and less picturesque buildings. Many of them stand in remote, inaccessible and little-known parts of the country; and their remarkable beauty, their historical associations and architectural merits, may have escaped the attention of many who love to explore the English countryside. It has therefore been deemed advisable to depict and to describe a series of typical examples taken from different counties and constructed of various materials, so that a record may be made ere many may entirely disappear. The manor-house is the principal dwelling-place in most villages, and to it the chief attention has been paid; but as this book is a study of the domestic architecture of the style of dwelling that ranked between the mansion and the farm or cottage, it has been thought well to illustrate the work by including some examples of a kindred nature that cannot be strictly included in the generic term manor-house.

It would have been an easy task to fill the volume with pictures and descriptions of well-known buildings that have often been photographed and sketched, and about which much has been written, but an attempt has been made to go outside the beaten track, the oft-trodden road, and to record the more unusual examples not so well known. The description of the details of the manor-houses of England has been given in plain language, as free as possible from technical terms ; and the subject has been treated for the purpose of interesting the general public rather than for the edification of the architectural expert.

The author desires to express his grateful thanks to Messrs. Batsford for much assistance they have rendered to him in the preparation of this book, and for their valuable advice and personal interest in the work ; also to the artist, Mr. Sydney Jones, for his descriptive notes on some of the houses which the writer had not an opportunity of personally visiting, and to Mrs. Arthur Stratton for kindly searching for some references in the British Museum with regard to the history of some of the manors.

P. H. DITCHFIELD.

BARKHAM RECTORY, BERKSHIRE,
January, 1910.

CONTENTS

CHAPTER		PAGE
I	INTRODUCTORY: THE MANOR-HOUSE	3
II	THE MANOR	11
III	THE EVOLUTION OF THE MANOR-HOUSE	17
IV	MATERIALS OF CONSTRUCTION	40
	STONE	46
	TIMBER	68
	BRICK	86
	FLINT	104
	PLASTER	106
V	EXTERIOR DETAILS	115
	CHIMNEYS	115
	PORCHES AND DOORS	121
	WINDOWS	129
	ROOFS AND GABLES	132
VI	INTERIOR DETAILS	141
	MANTELPIECES AND FIREPLACES	145
	STAIRCASES	153
	PANELLING	160
	CEILINGS	165
	WINDOWS	172
VII	METAL-WORK	176
	LEADWORK	176
	IRONWORK	180
VIII	GARDENS AND SURROUNDINGS	188
	INDEX	203

ST. CATHERINE'S COURT, NEAR BATH. FROM THE TERRACE

THE MANOR-HOUSES OF ENGLAND

I

INTRODUCTORY: THE MANOR-HOUSE

ENGLAND is remarkable for the number and beauty of the old country houses, set amid pleasant scenes, that abound in various parts of our island. Hidden away from the gaze of the multitude in sequestered villages and obscure hamlets, they are very humble-minded, very retiring. They do not court attention, these English manor-houses, or seek to attract the eye by glaring incongruities or obtrusive detail. They seem in quest of peace, and love obscurity. Hence few know how fair they are, how full of grace and charm, as they stand in their sweet old-fashioned gardens surrounded by rare blendings of art and nature in park and pleasance. They brood in their old age over many scenes of bygone history, over the memories of sire and grandsire and retain vivid recollections of the vigorous old squire and his lady who reared these walls in Tudor days and carefully saw to the carving of his and his dame's initials over the doorway—R. D. and E. D. 1595 A. D.

The builders of these houses were animated by that same spirit which moved Sir William Temple, cultured diplomatist, philosopher and garden lover, to write, "The greatest advantages men have by riches are, to give, to build, to plant and make pleasant scenes." And certainly they showed by their buildings that they were men of taste and refinement, very different from Macaulay's unflattering picture of the old English country squire who is represented as an ignorant boor. It is not in the greatest mansions, the vast piles erected by the great nobles of the court, enriched by the plunder of the monasteries, that we find such artistic perfections, but most often in the smaller manor-houses of the knights and squires. These are the buildings which delight us, the charms of which we are attempting to set forth in this book. The great noblemen and courtiers were filled with the desire for extravagant display, and erected such clumsy piles as Wollaton and Burghley House, importing Flemish and German artisans to load them with bastard Italian Renaissance detail. Nothing could be worse than some of these vast structures, with their distorted gables, their chaotic proportions and their crazy interpretation of classic orders. Contrast these vast piles with the typical Tudor manor-house, the means of the builders of which, or their good taste, would not permit of such a profusion of these architectural luxuries, and you will discover the far greater attractiveness of the humbler dwelling. It is unequalled in its combination of stateliness with homeliness, in its expression of the manner of life of the men who built it.

Such a noble Tudor house is Whittington Court in Gloucestershire in the delightful region of the Cotswolds. It is at once stately and homely, and its picturesqueness is in no way diminished by the Queen Anne addition with its conspicuous bay. Its three graceful gables, tall chimneys, and mullioned windows are worthy of the art of their Tudor builders.

These men built not only for themselves but for their sons and grandsons. They lighted what Ruskin calls the

WHITTINGTON COURT, GLOUCESTERSHIRE

Sixth Lamp of Architecture, the Lamp of Memory, and considered it an evil sign of a people for houses to be built to last for one generation only. They felt that

"having spent their lives happily and honourably, they would be grieved, at the close of them, to think that the plan of their earthly abode, which had seen, and seemed almost to sympathise in all their honour, their gladness or their suffering—that this, with all the record it bare of them, and all of material things that they had loved and ruled over, and set the stamp of themselves upon—was to be swept away, as soon as there was room made for them in the grave; that no respect was to be shown to it, no affection felt for it, no good to be drawn from it by their children; that though there was a monument in the church, there was no warm monument in the hearth and house to them; that all that they had ever treasured was despised, and the places that had sheltered and comforted them were dragged down to the dust. I say that a good man would fear this; and that, far more, a good son, a noble descendant, would fear doing this to his father's house. . . . When men do not love their hearths, nor reverence their thresholds, it is a sign that they have dishonoured both. . . . Our God is a household God as well as a heavenly one; He has an altar in every man's dwelling; let men look to it when they rend it lightly and pour out its ashes."[1]

Such feelings seem to have animated the builders of the gems of domestic architecture that adorn our country-side. They stamped their impress on the homes they reared. They expected their children to respect their gift to their families. They carved their names or their initials or their arms over their doorways. They adorned them with texts or homely verse, pious thoughts, or quaint or humorous conceits. They built surely and well so that their houses might last, not for their own pleasure nor for their own use, but for their descendants, who would thus venerate the hand that laid those stones and respect the memory of their forefathers and the honour of their house.

[1] Ruskin's *Seven Lamps of Architecture.*

BOTT'S GREEN HOUSE, NEAR SHUSTOKE, WARWICKSHIRE

We shall visit many such houses during our peregrinations. As an example of the long, low type of restful English manor-house we could not find a better instance than the curious half-timbered mansion known as Bott's Green House, near Shustoke, in Warwickshire. Its curved and slanting braces and its fine porch and entrance gate are charming features. It stands completely away from the busy haunts of men in the midst of an unspoilt country. The *fleur-de-lis* of the Digby family is very prominently inserted in the front. Within there is a carved stone mantelpiece carefully painted and grained to imitate wood, and upstairs a small panelled room of plain design.

In contrast with this peaceful abode is the Yorkshire manor-house of Lawkland Hall upon the borders of Lancashire, situated on the wild moorland that separates the two counties. It belongs to a different type, and has a stern rugged look which harmonizes well with its surroundings.

Time has wrought its ravages on many of these old houses. Families have lived and died out. Few, save the delver in old records, can tell the names for which those initials R. D. and E. D. stand. The golden stain of time gives light and colour to its architecture; but often ruin and decay have also left their marks. Reckless owners who love new things, new fashions and new styles, have doomed many of them to death. At the beginning of the last century there was a veritable rage for pulling down old mansions. You can still see the terraces of the garden, the old fishponds and possibly the moat, but the house has gone, a prey to the vandalism of the age. Others have succumbed to new inventions. Coal fires were unusual when the chimneys were built with a fatal beam running across their cavities. Hence fires have destroyed many of those ancient mansions which often stand in solitary state far from the nearest fire-engine station, and nothing is saved. Only a tithe is left of these pleasant houses. It is

LAWKLAND HALL, YORKSHIRE

well, therefore, to survey them before they vanish, to gather up the fragments that remain, to learn from them how to build surely and well, to avoid the construction of those "thin, tottering, foundationless shells of splintered wood and imitation stone," and to take as our models these beautiful dwellings that our sires have left us.

II

THE MANOR

WHAT is a manor-house? Evidently the house of the lord of the manor situated upon his estate. And what is a manor? Many chapters would be needed for the full discussion of the origin, growth and development of the English manor, its customs, laws and rights, and in spite of the researches of the learned there is still some obscurity on this subject, and all historians hold not the same views. I can only find space to refer very briefly to the story of the manor; but it is necessary to distinguish between the house so designated which gives the title to this book, and an ordinary house of a country gentleman who was not a manor-lord.

We can trace the manorial system back to its infancy in Celtic and Roman times, when "the Roman lordships and villas undoubtedly played their part as providing natural and powerful centres in the process of settlement and organization."[1] With the coming of the Saxon tribes who introduced the formation of village communities, hundreds and shires, the process of evolution developed. They formed tûns, or hams, or settlements, making clearings in the forests, subduing nature as they had subdued the British, and keeping together for the purpose of defending themselves against an enemy and for the better pursuit of

[1] *The Manor and Manorial Records*, by N. J. Hone, p. 6.

agriculture. How far these inhabitants of primitive settlements were free without the government of an over-lord, it is difficult to determine; but they needed a leader to organize their forces for war, a judge to decide their disputes, and in return for such services a lord began to receive dues and rents and labour on the part of his tenants. Under the Norman system of feudal tenure the manorial system developed, and manors were reorganized on a more strictly feudal basis. The lord became a very important person and ruled over his little kingdom, though his authority was by no means absolute. The tenants or villeins had their customary rights, and the lord was bound to observe them. He could levy fines in certain cases, a heriot or the best chattel belonging to a tenant's estate on death, and much else, and the tenants were obliged to work certain days on the lord's land. The lord used to hold his court, and the Court Rolls of numerous manors are in existence dating back to Edwardian times, and revealing many interesting features of old village life and property. The manor is an institution which, under varying forms and circumstances, has existed from a period "whereunto the memory of man runneth not to the contrary" till the present day. Of course the great feudal privileges which were formerly attached to the lord of the manor have passed into abeyance, but he is still a real factor in local life. As Mr. Hone tells us in his book, to which I have already referred, "Parish and district councils, in questions constantly arising touching village greens, recreation grounds, commons and rights of way, find that they have to reckon with him in the exercise of their newly acquired powers, and have to adjust their claims in accordance with the old manorial rights enjoyed by him and his predecessors for centuries."

The accompanying plan of a manor shows in the centre of the village the manor-house with the lord's demesne around it, and near it the church. The main street of the village leads to the river, and on each side are the houses of the tenants and the common pasture with crofts or small enclosures or grass yards for the rearing of calves and baiting farm stock; this was the common farmstead. The lord's mill stood by the river, where all the tenants were obliged to grind their corn. On the north lay the arable fields of the community divided into three large fields, in which the rotation of crops was strictly enforced, each field lying fallow once in three years. To each freeman was assigned his own family lots, which were scattered about in the open fields. Shots or furlongs were divisions of the open fields, "a furrow long," divided into strips or acres. Gored acres were strips in the open fields pointed at one end. Around the arable land were the waste and woodland used for the pasturage of pigs, and for the hunting of the lord. You can see him with his retainers in the plan sallying forth with his hounds on a hunting expedition. The remains of this common field system are still evident in many parts of the

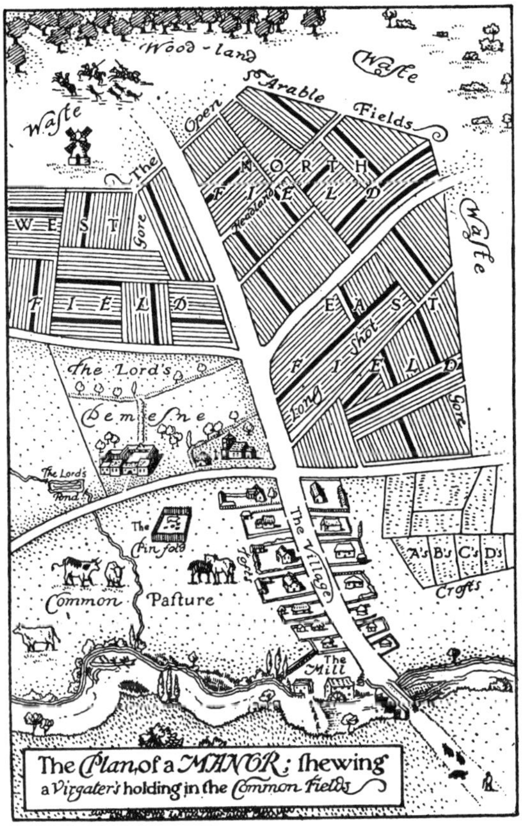

The Plan of a MANOR; ſhewing a Virgater's holding in the Common fields

country, the fields being termed "lot meadows" or "Lammas lands."

The best definition of a manor is, perhaps, that given by Mr. Scargill-Bird in his *Guide to the Public Records.* He states that a manor is "a certain circuit of ground granted by the king to some baron or man of worth as an inheritance for him and his heirs, with the exercise of such jurisdiction within the said compass as the king saw fit to grant, and subject to the performance of such services and yearly rents as were by the grant required." A manor is not coterminous with the parish. Sometimes a village is divided into as many as five manors, as at East Hendred, in Berkshire. The village of Sutton Courtenay has three manor-houses, two belonging to the same manor, and the third to quite a different property. Some manor-lords had many grants of lands and manors, and in their turn made grants of manors to less important persons. Thus, Finchampstead manor, which at an early date was divided into two manors, being granted by the owner, Sir William Banastre, to his two daughters, Constance and Agatha, was always held of the over-lord, the owner of Aldermaston manor. A process of sub-division of manors went on until the reign of Edward I, after which time no new manors were created.

The manor-house was, therefore, the hall of the lord of the manor. It was usually situated in the centre of the village on the demesne land and near the church and rectory. He did not always reside there. Sometimes it was inhabited by his bailiff or steward, and in the hall the manor-courts were held, justice administered and all the affairs of the community settled.

In later times when rich London merchants bought manors in the country, not content with the old houses they found there, they reared more magnificent edifices. This was the case at Campden, in Gloucestershire, and a view of this fine estate is given in the illustration. The manor was bought in 1609 by Sir Baptist Hicks, sometime Lord Mayor of London, who soon began to build this large mansion on the high ground overlooking the vale to the south of the church. The view, taken from a curious coloured drawing in the British Museum, shows the palace with its forecourt and

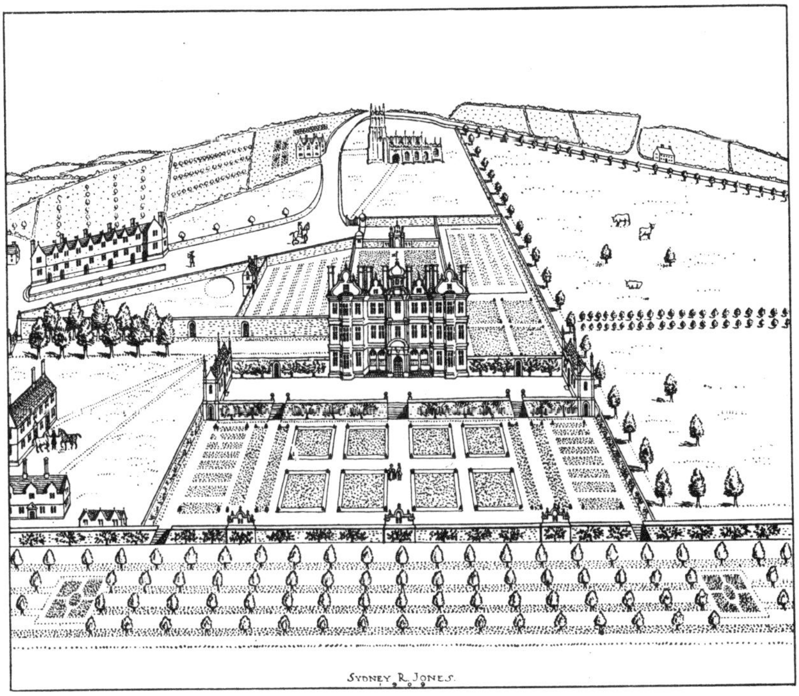

CHIPPING CAMPDEN HOUSE, GLOUCESTERSHIRE
From an early coloured drawing

grounds and gardens. Unfortunately it was partly destroyed during the Civil War, and only two pavilions, the entrance gate, and the almonry remain to tell of its former magnificence.

The manor-house played an important part in the life of the village, and is an interesting feature of every parish, both historically and architecturally. Much attention in late years has been given to the tracing of the manorial history of each manor and parish. It is, as the writer knows from painful experience, a surprisingly difficult task, in spite of the researches which have been made at the Record Office and amongst other stores of ancient documents. But the labour is sometimes rewarded by interesting glimpses of mediæval or Elizabethan life, by happy acquaintance with bygone worthies, quarrelsome lords and unyielding tenants, and by the light which such documents throw on the history of the country. Manorial histories always must have a fascination for the student of our ancient manners and customs.

III

THE EVOLUTION OF THE MANOR-HOUSE

OUR main concern is with the architectural charms and beauties of the English manor-house, its details, its garden, the well-wrought gates, its varying materials. We are trying to describe the attractive features that remain, and need not concern ourselves with its origin and evolution. Nevertheless, the construction and plan of many a manor-house are based upon the Gothic traditions of early times; some few of the houses that remain are the actual mediæval structures of the early lords. It will, therefore, be necessary to describe briefly an original type of the early residence of the manor-lord, and trace its development.

The earliest house in Saxon times consisted of a capacious hall wherein the lord and his retainers feasted during the day and where the latter slept at night, the lord retiring to an adjoining chamber for repose. Besides, there was a buttery, and around the house were lean-to roofs covering a stable, barn and offices. A very simple arrangement this which continued for some centuries. The house was thatched with reeds or straw or roofed with wooden shingles. Little change was made when the Normans came. The main apartment was the hall, and Alexander Necham tells us that in addition to this there were at the end of the twelfth century the private or bedchamber, the kitchen, the larder, the sewery and the cellar. Sandon manor-house, in Essex, in the twelfth century, had a hall, a bower or women's apartment, a latrina, besides barns, wash-house, cowshed, brewery, sty and henhouse. Kensworth manor had a *domus* or entrance, a bower and a large hall, besides the usual outbuildings. Even the palaces of the King at Clarendon, Kennington, Woodstock and elsewhere contained no additional accommodation except a chapel. The private or bedchamber, called a solar, was situated on the second storey, the room beneath being used as a cellar. The fire burned in the middle of the hall, and the smoke escaped through a hole in the roof. In the solar there were fireplaces and a chimney-piece remains in a house at Boothby Pagnell. In early times the cooking was performed at the fire in the centre of the hall; later on there was a separate kitchen with an open roof. The windows of the house were narrow slits and could be closed by wooden shutters.

The manor-house at Appleton, Berkshire, belongs to the end of the twelfth century. It is surrounded by a moat, and is of a simple oblong plan, three doorways, round-headed with early English mouldings, being the only parts which retain the original character.

Boothby Pagnell manor-house, in Lincolnshire, is a good example of a twelfth-century building, of which two views are given. It consists of a large hall with windows high up in the wall, one of which is a later addition. It was the seat of a family named Boothby, the heiress of which married a Paynell. Newport Pagnell, in Buckinghamshire, also belonged to the Paynells, but Leland states that they had "a great mynde to ly at Boutheby [i.e. to be buried there] wher they had a praty stone house withyn a mote." Traces of the moat still remain, and also the stone house as a memorial of an old Norman dwelling.

The plan of these buildings with barns and other outbuildings was in the form of a quadrangle. The barns were

BOOTHBY PAGNELL MANOR-HOUSE
VIEWS AND PLANS

of great size. Several fourteenth-century barns are still in existence and are like large churches with nave and aisles. Gunthwaite Hall barn, near Penistone, is 165 ft. long, 43 ft. broad and 30 ft. high.[1] We like to picture the life of the inhabitants of these primitive manor-houses, the lady sitting with her maids working their tapestry with figures of swans and beasts and ships and heroes, the playing of games in the courtyard, the men returning from their hunting, feasting in the hall, the minstrels and jugglers contributing to their amusement. Padley Hall, in Derbyshire, is a good example of an ancient manor-house. The main building consisted of a hall and buttery on the ground floor, and above on the first floor was a chapel with a bower, and other buildings were grouped around an oblong courtyard.

As an example of this grouping of buildings round an oblong courtyard an illustration is given of a picturesque house in Somerset, though of a later date. It stands about midway between Yeovil and Montacute, and is called the manor house of Preston Bermondsey, often described as Preston Plucknett. Its name suggests that it belonged to the monks of Bermondsey Priory, but if that be so their possession was not of long duration. Its second name is derived from Alan de Plugenet, an early lord of the manor, which was owned in the early half of the fifteenth century by one John Stourton, who built this house. On the right of the view you see the original hall with a porch leading to the screens. The windows are Decorated. At the dais end of the hall you will notice the lowering of the sill of the window, giving it an importance which later was further enhanced by the use of the bay or oriel window generally found in this position.[2] An old sketch drawn prior to the alterations shows that some changes have been made

[1] *Evolution of the English House*, by S. O. Addy.

[2] *Domestic Architecture of the Tudor Period*, by Garner and Stratton, Part I, p. 25.

PRESTON PLUCKNETT, SOMERSET

in the part of the house on the left of the porch. The octagonal chimney is a fine example of the type which prevailed for some time when the disuse of the louvre was becoming general. You will notice the great breadth of the wall on which it stands, due to the depth of the fireplace within. Disfiguring brickwork has been inserted in the original outlets for the smoke at the sides of the upper part of the shaft. The interior of the house has been much altered, and the interest and beauty of the building lie in the long restful lines of the stone-built exterior, and are enhanced by the noble barn which is a few years later than the house, but erected by the same owner, John Stourton. It would be difficult to find a more picturesque group of buildings.

The thirteenth-century manor-house differs little from its predecessor. You can see a good example at Charney Basset in Berkshire, which has as its chief feature the hall, and the chambers at each side are arranged as wings, so as to form with the hall three sides of a quadrangular courtyard. A chapel or oratory adjoins the solar in the south wing. A curious representation of a manor-house of this period is shown on a personal seal of the date 1273, reproduced in the *Archæological Journal.*[1] It was constructed of wood with the exception of its cylindrical chimney-shaft; the windows of the solar are placed high on the left, and the doorway is on the right leading to the hall. The manor-house of the Greys, at Coggs, in Oxfordshire, is partly of this period, as is also that of Cottisford in the same county.

As an illustration of a fourteenth-century manor-house we give two views of Lower Brockhampton Hall, the interior of the ancient hall with its noble roof and minstrel gallery, and the exterior with the gatehouse. It stands in a hollow, and close to the ruins of a chapel of still earlier date. It is no longer the manor-house, that honour being held by the

[1] Vol. I, p. 219.

INTERIOR OF THE HALL, LOWER BROCKHAMPTON, HEREFORDSHIRE

eighteenth-century building which stands on high ground looking down on the beautiful old brick and timber house which is still almost surrounded by a moat. It is many a year since the family of Brockhampton, who took their name from the property, sold the manor. About the middle of the sixteenth century it was acquired by the Barneby family, one of whom suffered severely in the Civil Wars, and was accordingly compensated by being named for the intended Order of the Royal Oak. The detached gatehouse with its heavily studded door and the moat are relics of an earlier day when the only approach to the house lay through a drawbridge. This gatehouse, which, with the well-known one at Stokesay, is one of the very few timber ones existing in the country, is very early, and belongs to the closing years of the fourteenth century. The closeness of the upright timbers, the moulded board covering the ends of the joists, the carved bracket at the angles and the barge-boards all point to a good old age which retains the beauties of youth.

In the fourteenth century a greater desire for privacy was manifested in the multiplication of rooms, and houses were made much more convenient. The hall remained the principal apartment, and usually occupied the whole central portion of the house. Sometimes it extended from the floor to the roof; in other instances there were cellars or low rooms under it. In houses of this and of the preceding centuries, when the roof was too large to be covered by a single span, pillars of wood or stone were used to support it.

The following description[1] of the squire's house of the fifteenth and sixteenth centuries records their chief characteristics :—

"In the southern districts of England the old English manor-houses, the houses of the gentry generally, as well as

[1] *Surrey Archæological Collections*, a Paper on Timber Houses, by Charles Baily.

LOWER BROCKHAMPTON HALL

of the better class of yeomanry, were very simple in the plan, and very often exhibited a singular uniformity of design. In the centre was the hall, at the end of one side of which was the principal entrance to the house, a portion of the hall being cut off by a screen, to form a passage through the house from the front entrance to that at the back, which was directly opposite. On the side of this passage (known by the name 'the entrye,' and sometimes called the 'screens') and opposite to the screen were generally three doorways, as at Crowhurst Place, the seat of the Gaynesfords; sometimes, however, there were but two, as in the case at Great Tangley, in the parish of Wonersh in Surrey. In both these examples the first of these doors opens into a parlour; at Crowhurst the second leads to a staircase, and the third to the butteries, kitchen, and to the whole of the domestic offices.

"In the screen were two openings, without doors, through which the hall was entered. Beyond the upper or dais end of the hall were one or several rooms, of a more private character than either the parlour or hall; the sleeping-rooms were generally in the upper storeys. Externally there was usually a recess in the centre of the front, formed by one side of the hall, as we find was the case in the house of Great Tangley, as originally built. At either end of this central recess was a gable projection; the one forming a porch over the entrance, the other a bay-window to the hall. Beyond these were two larger gabled ends, one enclosing the parlour and offices, and the other the more private rooms before noticed."

If in these examples the parlour was on the side of the screens remote from the dais end of the hall, the arrangement was exceptional. An examination of numerous plans and an inspection of mediæval houses prove that the servants' quarters—the kitchen, butteries, bakehouses, brewhouse—were always grouped at one end of the hall, and the rooms of the family—the parlour, solar, and bedrooms—at the other. This plan continued until the time of Inigo Jones, when the hall had quite ceased to be the centre of the

CROWHURST PLACE, SURREY, SHOWING MOAT AND FOOTBRIDGE

life of the household and had become merely an entrance or a passage. The illustration of Ditcheat shows the ancient arrangement of the entrance to the hall, the screens, passage, and buttery hatch. We shall refer again to this beautiful house in the chapter relating to Interior Details (p. 141).

The early Tudor period, which commenced about the middle of the fifteenth century and lasted until about the year 1540, brought into being many charming manor-houses as well as the palaces of kings and the mansions of the nobles. Hitherto each Englishman's house was literally his castle, and needed defences and the means of resisting an attack. It was girt by a protecting moat and often was built around a courtyard with strong guarding gates and towers. But with the cessation of prolonged wars and internal strife, and a more settled state of the country, the need of such protection passed away, until at length in Elizabethan times defences were practically disregarded. As early as the reign of Henry VI we find a country squire built his manor-house at Great Chalfield, in Wiltshire, without considering it necessary to fortify his dwelling beyond giving it a moat.

In the time of Henry VII the country became thoroughly settled. The country gentlemen became wealthy owing to the sale of their rich fleeces to the clothiers. They set themselves to add to, or to build anew, the ill-planned and inconvenient manor-houses bequeathed to them by their forefathers. A little later the after-gleaning of the spoils of the monasteries added to their wealth and increased their lust for "bricks and mortar."

Then arose some of the most perfect examples of English domestic architecture that our land ever possessed. The style was essentially English. Though Henry VIII brought over foreign artificers, who were employed to assist in the construction of his palaces and in designing decorations for the mansions of the great, the native masons and builders were engaged on these lesser houses, and wrought in simple

DITCHEAT PRIORY, SOMERSET

fashion, clinging to the traditional style which they had loved and reverenced. Moreover, the squire and owner took a personal and active interest in the work. This personal care and interest was observable in the building of many houses, in many periods. See the accurate accounts and minute superintendency of the building of Longleat by Sir John Thynne.

We like to read of the leisurely way in which Chastleton House (*v.* p. 193) was restored by the squire, John Jones, in the eighteenth century. The work was all done very gradually and very thoroughly. The stone was seasoned for three years, first under sheds, and then in the open, and the squire exercised close supervision over his workmen. After they had left work for the day he used to go and try if he could pick the mortar out with his knife; if he succeeded, the work had to be pulled to pieces next day and done over again.

When we, in these days, wish to build a house, we engage an architect. We tell him some of our ideas and vague notions, but we leave the whole matter in his hands. We order a house as we would order a motor-car or a portmanteau. The Tudor squire himself superintended the building, watched the laying of each stone and beam, paid the workmen, kept the accounts, arranged the plans and the conveniences of the house according to his liking, and cared not to copy classical models or foreign details. He clung with whole-hearted affection to the old English style of building, which he considered best suited to the national character and climate. His son, or grandson, followed in his footsteps, preserved the tradition of building, added to the house, making improvements and alterations according to his own taste and ideas. Hence houses sprang up showing no unity of design with picturesque grouping of portions erected at different times. They were in the early Tudor period usually built round a court with a substantial entrance gateway, sometimes carried up to form a tower. Fulham Palace, or, as it is more correctly named, the Bishop's manor-house at Fulham, built in the time of Henry VII, is a good example of this. We admire the mullioned windows, the parapets corbelled out and battlemented, the irregular and picturesque grouping of the various parts of these old Tudor houses. Sometimes we find a great mixture of material, stone, brick, wood and plaster ; but the great hall remains as the principal feature with its screen, dais, bay window and huge fireplace in one of the side walls.

The accompanying plans will reveal more clearly this development and evolution of the house than any description can give. We see in the plan of the house at Warneford the simplest form of the hall and offices. It was the manor-house of the St. John family, now quite ruined. Two rows of tall pillars carried the principal timbers of the roof. The Norman plan of Boothby Pagnell (p. 19) shows a plain oblong house divided into a large and a small chamber. The chief apartment is on the first floor, reached by the steps illustrated, with a vaulted undercroft beneath. The second plan, that of the typical fifteenth-century manor-house of Wanswell Court, Gloucestershire, shows the addition of several chambers. In addition to the central hall, there is a room at each end, a large kitchen, and a cellar. The apartment at the west end was a parlour, and it is clear that the lord dined there, and not in the common hall.

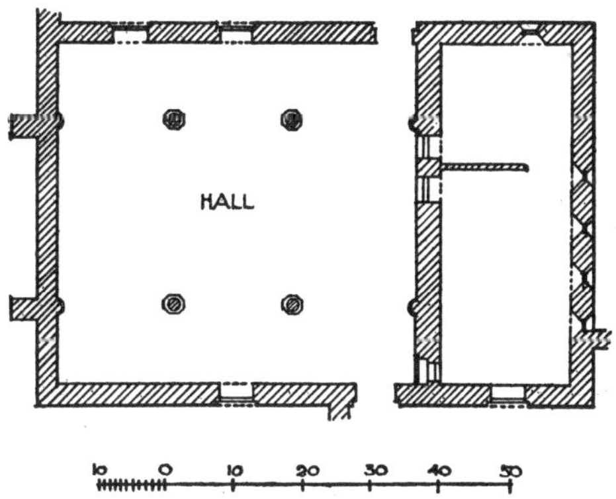

PLAN OF AN EARLY HOUSE AT WARNEFORD, HAMPSHIRE

The third plan reveals a further development. It shows

the manor-house of Great Chalfield with its outbuildings, moat, and the adjoining church. The hall still retains its dominant position, but the number and complexity of the subordinate rooms have increased. In the chapter on Gardens (p. 193) is illustrated the plan of the Elizabethan house at Chastleton, built round a small court, which shows the greatly advanced ideas of comfort and privacy which had grown up with the sixteenth century.

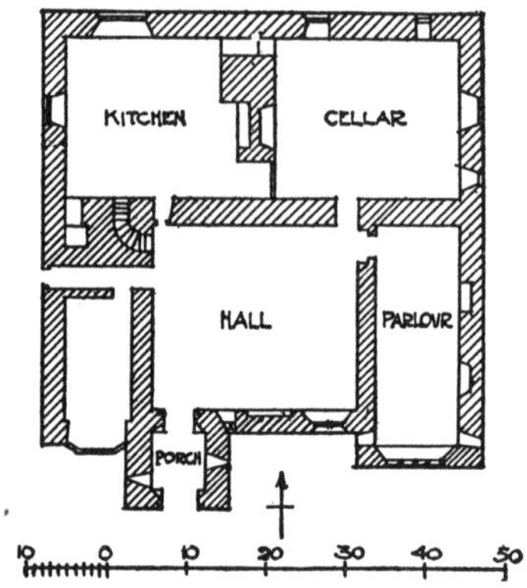

PLAN OF WANSWELL COURT, GLOUCESTERSHIRE

Dr. Andrew Boorde, whose *Dyatary of Helth* was published in 1542, tells how and "under what manner and fashion a man shulde buylde his howse or mansyon in exchewyng thynges the whiche shulde shorten the lyfe of man." He advocates the need of a good soil and good prospect. The air must be pure, frisky and clean, the foundations on gravel mixed with clay. The chief prospects should be east and west, or north-east and south-west ; never south, for the south wind doth corrupt and make evil vapours. This advice accords with that of a contemporary poet, who asserts

> The south as unkind draweth sickness too near,
> The north as a friend maketh all again clear.

"Make the hall," he says, "under such a fashion that the parlour be annexed to the head of the hall, and the buttery and pantry be at the lower end of the hall ; the cellar under the pantry, set somewhat above from the buttery and pantry, coming with an entry by the wall of the buttery ; the pastry-house and larder-house annexed to the kitchen. Then divide the lodgings by the circuit of the quadrivial court, and let the gatehouse be opposite, or against the hall door (not directly) but the hall door standing abase, and the gatehouse in the middle of the front entering into the place. Let the privy chamber be annexed to the great chamber of estate with other chambers necessary for the building, so that many of the chambers may have a prospect into the chapel." He locates the stables, slaughterhouse and dairy a quarter of a mile away from the house, and advises that the moat should be divers times scoured and kept clean from mud and weeds. The advice of the good doctor seems to have been very sound, and much needed in the infant days of sanitary science.

In the Elizabethan house we notice great attempts towards formal arrangement. No defence works were needed, and in the spacious days of good Queen Bess there was evinced a desire for display and magnificence as well as for comfort and convenience. Small suites of rooms were erected for guests on one side of the court, each room opening into the other, and the long gallery, a familiar feature of an Elizabethan house, was formed on the first floor of the left-hand side of the court. The windows became larger. The **H**-shaped type of house was evolved, which is only the old plan of the hall in the centre flanked on one side by the family apartments, on the other by those of the servants. Also the **E**-shaped type came into fashion, erroneously supposed to have been invented as a compliment to the Virgin Queen. Of course it is only the hall with wings projecting on one side only, the central stroke of the letter representing the porch.

We shall give examples in subsequent chapters of the details of these houses, the Renaissance characteristics and changes in fashion which were introduced.

With the beginning of the seventeenth century the "dining parlour" came into vogue, and the old fashion of the family and household meeting in the common hall fell into desuetude. Henceforward the servants adopted the custom of "keeping themselves to themselves," quite in accordance with modern notions.

The Jacobean house is but a further development of the Elizabethan. Artists became more imbued with the Italian spirit, and we notice an increased profusion of ornament, wonderful plastered ceilings and elaborately carved panels

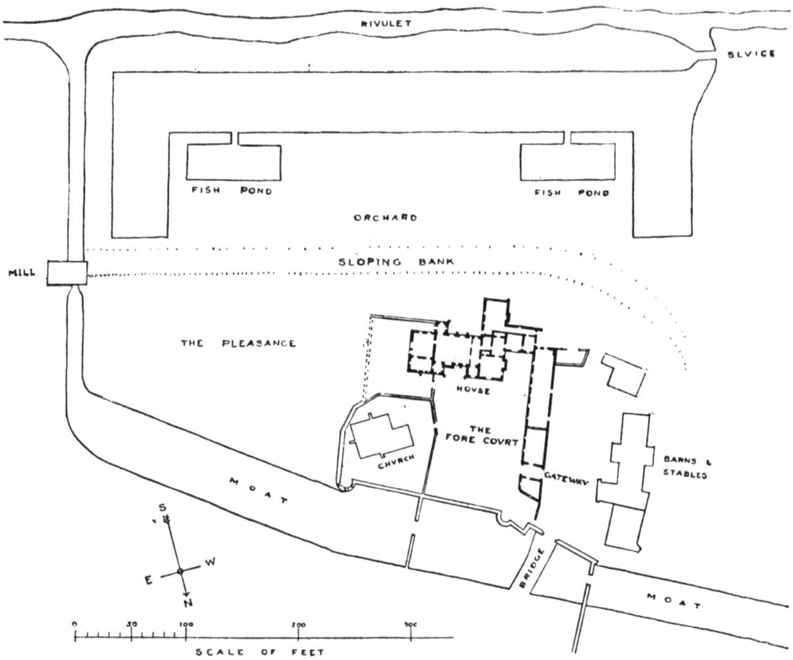

PLAN OF THE HOUSE AND ITS SURROUNDINGS
GREAT CHALFIELD MANOR, WILTSHIRE

and mantelpieces. The Tudor style became more and more Italianized, though it still retained many of its English characteristics. Evidences of foreign influence are seen in the work of Thorpe, Robert and Huntingdon Smithson. Then came the era of the "English Palladio," Inigo Jones, who acquired his knowledge at Venice and in Denmark, accompanied Anne of Denmark, the queen of James I, to England, and became the surveyor-general of the royal buildings under that monarch and his son Charles. Though his work was mainly concerned with royal and noble houses, such as the Banqueting House Whitehall, Stoke Park, Wilton House, and St. John's College, Oxford, his influence and that of his pupil Webb extended itself in the country, especially in decoration, and the various rooms of the richer manor-lords were converted into, as Bacon described them, "delicate and rich cabinets, daintily paved, richly hanged, glazed with crystalline glass, and all other elegancy that may be thought of." The golden age of English house-building had passed, and it was left to the humbler building, the smaller manor-houses, the yeoman's house, and country cottages to maintain in some measure the traditions of English Gothic and Tudor art. Sir Christopher Wren lent his influence to the furtherance of Renaissance ideals, though his art differed from the Palladian adaptations of Inigo Jones. It is true that his successors broke away from his manner in large and important buildings, but his influence lived on, and is seen in the quieter domestic building which constituted the English vernacular for many a day.

Lower Lypiatt, in Gloucestershire, is a good example of an early eighteenth-century house. It was erected in 1717, and we can detect the strong classic influence of the successors of Wren. The house is set back in a forecourt bounded by stone piers and wrought-iron railings.

The gates are extremely good and have a lock-rail of richly interlacing work showing German influence. The maker of this ironwork was Warren, who wrought it for Judge Coxe, the builder of the house. Warren was the artificer of many handsome gates of that period, including those at Trinity College, Cambridge; Eagle House, Clapton; the Little Cloister by Westminster Abbey; Abney House, Stoke Newington; and Burleigh House at Enfield. The last closely resemble those at Lower Lypiatt, having four small panels, each filled with four scrolls proceeding from a circle, united by vertical bars, with the central panel formed of scrolls and water-leaves. The horizontals are fringed with C scrolls holding waved spikes and the dog-bars are arrow-pointed. The low pyramid tops of the piers are crowned by solid vases. Master Warren and his brother blacksmiths of the eighteenth century were wonderful artists.

With the commencement of the eighteenth century was evolved the so-called "Queen Anne" style, which has given us many charming and picturesque houses throughout the country. As the late Mr. J. J. Stevenson wrote :—

> "Brick had become the common material of the country, and the classic forms and mouldings the vernacular of the workmen, who following, apparently, their own instincts, formed the style out of these elements, without drawings from architects, who were too learned to tolerate its barbarism. The shaping of the gables into various curves, which is one of the characteristics of the style, is a simple and natural, and consequently cheap, mode of producing an effect in brick. It is one of the many ways in which the builders in every country, still inspired by the old Gothic freedom, got rid of the trammels of classic rule."[1]

We might pass on to think of the Georgian builders, of the work of the brothers Adam and other great masters, but that would carry us beyond the limits of our search. As an illustration of the later development of house-building we give a view of the manor-house of Studley, in Warwickshire. The chimneys that once soared high have hidden themselves behind a parapet. The rows of plain oblong windows are scarcely attractive, and the redeeming feature of the house is the splendid iron-work of the gates, which are worthy of a better dwelling. It is with the old manor-houses of England that we are concerned, and compared with them modern or comparatively modern work seems unsatisfying and unsatisfactory. All

[1] *English House Architecture*, I, 331.

LOWER LYPIATT HOUSE (ON THE COTSWOLDS), GLOUCESTERSHIRE

these old houses seem to us beautiful. Time has added to their charm. Some are more beautiful than others, but there are no failures ; and though Time has improved their appearance, mellowed their brickwork, wrought wonders on their tiled roofs, and cast over them the glamour of romance, their beauties are due to the skill and natural sense of artistic

STUDLEY MANOR-HOUSE, WARWICKSHIRE

effect of the village masons and artificers, carpenters, and smiths, who "built houses and churches such as for excellence and accuracy in architectural style we vainly now, with all our knowledge, attempt to imitate." Such is the sad confession of a modern architect. The examples of the work of these village artists, which we have selected for this book, are a witness to their skill. They wrought in various materials, and in the following chapters we will examine their work more closely, and delight ourselves by the contemplation. We shall try to trace the development of their ideas, as generation after generation they were striving after a more excellent way, to admire their efforts to make the houses beautiful inside and out, and to understand their conceptions of ornamentation and decoration. Perhaps we shall discover that our best ideals for future work will be formed by studying the triumphs of our native English craftsmen rather than in following the imaginings of alien builders unsuited to our climate and foreign to our traditions.

IV

MATERIALS OF CONSTRUCTION

IT has often been remarked how well the buildings bequeathed to us by our forefathers harmonize with their surroundings. They seem to be part of the landscape. There is no incongruity, no false or startling note. The cause of this harmonious blending is not hard to discover. Our ancestors always used the materials which Nature herself supplied in the neighbourhood wherein the house was to be reared. If they lived in a region of stone quarries, they constructed their houses of stone. If they were surrounded by woods and forests, the giant trees supplied them with timber for their dwellings. This was entirely in accordance with the eternal fitness of things. The half-timbered houses of Berkshire, Sussex or Kent would look out of place amid the wild moors of Yorkshire, where the stone hewn from the native quarries supplies fit and pleasing material for north-country dwellings. Compare the illustrations of two specimens of these types given opposite and on p. 43. The mediæval masons and their descendants worked unconsciously in accordance with this principle of æsthetic art. There were no railways to bring stone from far-off quarries, or slates from Wales, or bricks from Bracknell. Some of our kings delighted to bring Caen stone from Normandy by sea for great castles or abbeys. "Cane stone" was brought to Reading Abbey by Henry I and to Wallingford Castle, and when these great buildings were ruined the same stones were shipped off in barges for the improvement of Windsor Castle.

ST. BENEDICT'S PRIORY, NEAR TENTERDEN, KENT

But the builders of our manor-houses would not be inclined to incur the expense of bringing stone from Normandy. With here and there an exception, such as Shrub Place, Sussex, where Caen stone is used for the sixteenth-century addition, they used the materials that lay ready to hand, and thus avoided the production of strange anomalies and the association together of those constituent parts that Nature had not blended. They wrought as they best could, naturally, unaffectedly, and built for themselves those pleasing and enduring houses which it is our pleasure to admire and study and perhaps to do our best to imitate.

The external appearance of these buildings was in a great measure determined by the situation of the land upon which they stood and the materials it yielded, these factors also bearing the impress of the individual character of those who used them. Up and down the country-side is everywhere seen the work of these village craftsmen, vernacular work unaffected by imported design. It shows how local traditions of taste were cultivated and carried down from generation to generation. The builders of the smaller manor-houses and humbler cottages pursued the even tenor of their way, one age content to profit by the experience of its predecessor. Hence traditions in building arose from the long retention of certain definite tendencies, gradually gaining in power by the introduction of new methods and ideas. Villages or districts were self-centred, owing to the difficulties of communication and transit, and different parts of the country preserved their own peculiarities little affected by what was being accomplished in other parts of the country outside their own little world. Some wrought in stone, others in brick, plaster or timber; but the same underlying principle governed all—a wish to do their best with the materials nearest to hand. Such was the process; the results, though not without fault, command our admiration and respect.

Building materials naturally vary with the geological forma-

CARK HALL, LANCASHIRE

tion of our island, and determine the character of the great building districts. In the south-eastern region of England,

A GABLE AT SARRE, KENT

including Kent, Surrey, Sussex and eastern Hampshire, the natural materials are chiefly chalk, chalk marl and weald clay. Flints are often found in the chalk. The gable at Sarre shows the local use of brick. Originally the land was densely overgrown with forests. Thus we find the buildings composed of timber and plaster, of brick and flint, the houses being tile-hung or weather-boarded. This chalk formation continues through portions of the counties of Wilts and Berks and away to the sea coast of Suffolk. Chalk is the chief influence in the buildings, and plaster is commonly used, either separately or together with the other products of the land, flint and stone, bricks made from the clay and timber from the forest lands. The extreme easterly part of England, Essex, Norfolk, Suffolk and Kent, with the Isle of Thanet, yields clay for brickmaking and tiles. The great forest of Epping, stretching across Essex, was also important for its timber and contributed materials for the structure of the houses.

In the southern parts of Hampshire and Dorset, together with the Isle of Wight, we find chalk and flint. The great stone bed of oolite and lias, stretching from the Dorset coast in the south to the Yorkshire coast in the north, furnished most excellent building stone, and along its course is the region of the best stone buildings in the country. Cornwall, Devon and West Somerset produce granite, sandstone, grit and slate. With the Midlands as a centre, its arms stretching north, south and west, is the great sandstone formation. Almost all this land was thickly wooded. Hence this was pre-eminently the great timber-building district of England. The natural products of the north country are sandstone, limestone and granite which were used for the construction of houses in that district.

We will now study some of the beautiful works of art wrought in these various materials that Time has spared. It is impossible in this work to describe all the manor-houses in England, and we can only select typical examples fashioned of stone or timber, brick or flint or plaster ; but from these specimens we can judge of the achievements of the skill of our forefathers and admire their perfections.

THE MANOR-HOUSES OF ENGLAND

I. Stone

We must look for the best examples of stone buildings along the course of that broad band of oolite and lias which extends from the southern coast of Dorset to where the North Sea laves the shore of Yorkshire. It embraces part of Wiltshire, Somerset, Oxfordshire, Northamptonshire, Derbyshire, part of Lincolnshire. Along its course can be seen many of the most superb of English architectural triumphs, fine church towers and spires, some of our grandest cathedrals, such as Salisbury, Wells, Lincoln and Southwell, and beautiful stone manor-houses, mansions and cottages. It embraces the region of the Cotswolds, celebrated for its architectural beauties, and many other districts that abound in charming examples of exquisite construction.

In the southern counties of Somerset, Wilts and Dorset the buildings betray a strong mediæval influence. Gothic feeling probably lingered here longer than elsewhere in England, and some of the mediæval manor-houses happily remain, though many have fallen from their former state. There is a delightful old manor-house near Darleigh, in West Somerset, known variously as Bur or West Bower Manor, or Court, now called West Bower Farm, which is of very early construction, and belongs to the Decorated period of English architecture. Its entrance, guarded by two towers with windows far from the ground (those on the right and left of the entrance were evidently inserted in later times), shows that it was built in troublous days when the need of fortification had not passed away and when every Englishman's house was his castle. Probably the lean-to roof and present doorway are not part of the original building. It claims to be the birthplace of Jane Seymour, afterwards queen of Henry VIII and the mother of Edward VI. Her father, Sir John Seymour, was lord of the manor of Bur. The stone turrets still contain some of the old glass in

WEST BOWER FARM, NEAR DARLEIGH, WEST SOMERSET

which appear formal roses and archaic letters. M can be deciphered, and it probably stands for Malet.[1]

Perched high on a hillside stands the sturdy stone-built manor-house called Stanton Old Hall, in Derbyshire, within a short distance from Haddon Hall, commanding one of the loveliest views in the county. Its long, low front rising above the narrow flagged and terraced forecourt, its square-headed mullioned and latticed windows, and its gables finished with ball finials, suggest that it was built in the latter half of the sixteenth century, during the tenure of the Bache family. The family of the De Stantons was an ancient one. Robert de Stanton requested, in 1327, King Edward III to grant pontage to the men of Stanton and Swarkeston towards the repair of the bridge between the two towns. Fate has grimly distinguished the change of possession of this manor by the extinction, not infrequently by violence, of the male line of each family who has owned it from the thirteenth to the nineteenth century.[2]

The present tenant, a farmer of the name of Smith, claims that the house has been the home of his family for many generations past, and the sword of his great-great-great-grandfather hangs in the inglenook of the kitchen, where the massive oak ceiling beams and panelling on the low walls give an old-world character to the room.

A modern drawing-room has been added in recent times, and altogether the other sides of the house have lost their original character, but traces of the sloping garden suggest that the scheme must once have been very complete for a small house.

It is now the property of the Duke of Rutland. The site of the house forced the development of the plan. You will notice the graceful gables, the mullioned windows, the picturesque chimney-stack, the low pitch of the roof necessi-

[1] Fletcher Moss, *Pilgrimages to Old Houses.*

[2] Tilley, *Old Halls and Families of Derbyshire.*

STANTON OLD HALL, DERBYSHIRE

tated by the use of the heavy Derbyshire slabs. Our forefathers soon discovered that though steeply pitched roofs drained off the rain best, and were most satisfactory when thatch or light slates or tiles were used as roofing material, yet when heavy tiles or slabs were hung they pulled sorely on the rafters and broke the pegs that held them ; hence our ancestors wisely adopted a lower pitch. As you enter the house you notice that the door is fastened in the old-fashioned way—a great beam shot into holes in the wall. The hall is original, the furniture just the same as when the manor-lord sat at the head of the table, settled the disputes of his tenants, and dispensed common-sense justice at his court leet.

Sandford Orcas Manor-house, Dorset, is a good example of an early sixteenth-century stone house. A view of the fine Tudor gatehouse is shown. The house is built of Ham Hill stone, to which local material the old houses of Dorset and Somerset owe not a little of their mellow colouring and beautiful texture. It has two storeys, with rooms above in the attics, having mullioned windows with dripstones in the gables. It is entered by a beautiful porch which leads to the screens on the west of the hall. The hall has a large bay mullioned window. On the summit of the three gables are curious grotesque figures. The porch has a chamber over it, an elaborately carved coat-of-arms over the door, and finely carved finials crown the buttresses on each side of the porch.

On the borders of Yorkshire and Derbyshire at Holmesfield, not far from Sheffield, stands the lonely Cartledge Hall, far from the haunts of men, a manor-house of the late fifteenth or early sixteenth century. Few people know of the existence of this. It is built throughout of large blocks of stone, and has the typical large stone slabs common to the district. It stands solitary and alone, exposed to the fierce storms that sweep over a wild, bleak

THE GATEHOUSE, SANDFORD ORCAS, DORSETSHIRE

and rugged moor, challenging the fury of the tempestuous gales. With its bold unimaginative details and bleak surroundings the house seems to convey to the mind the stern spirit of the north-country man, his steadiness, his practical nature and strength of character. Some of the interior details which are of much interest will be examined later. The house remains a good type of a northerner's rugged dwelling.

CARTLEDGE HALL, DERBYSHIRE

A Yorkshire type is seen at Oakwell Hall, Birstall, near Leeds, though a century later than Cartledge, having been built in 1583 by one Henry Batt, of whom nothing good can be said save that he had the good taste to build this noble dwelling. Its narrow mullioned windows and somewhat heavy appearance correspond to the usual features of Yorkshire houses. Its interest is that it is almost in the same condition as when Henry Batt finished it, a quaint homestead with a panelled hall, huge fireplace, a gallery running round the chamber and old dog-gates at the foot of the stairs to prevent the animals gaining access to the

OAKWELL HALL, YORKSHIRE

bedrooms. The founder achieved ignoble fame by waging war against the vicar, appropriating money that had been entrusted to him for building a school, selling the great bell at Birstall and pulling down the vicarage. His successors had to pay heavily for this sacrilege. You can see a bloody footprint in one of the bedrooms imprinted by the ghost of a Batt who was slain in a duel in London. The Fearnleys used to make the old house echo with sounds of merriment and hunting songs, but its chief fame is derived from its association with Charlotte Brontë, who pictured its ancient gables and old-world charm in *Shirley*.

Of stone manor-houses dating from the days of Elizabeth we have many other examples. Owlpen in Gloucestershire presents many features of peculiar interest.

The parish of Owlpen has been aptly described by an eighteenth-century writer[1] as a "kind of gloomy retreat," and the manor-house itself is in keeping with its surroundings. Shut in by steep hills and hidden in trees, access to it is most difficult, the more so because of the state of the roads. When reached, the weird beauty of the place gives an impression not easily shaken off. It is indeed something of a relief to learn that the present owner does not live in the grey old house, but uses it and the beautiful gardens —by daylight—as a picnic place. The house itself, which is built of the stone of the county, is a specially interesting example of sixteenth-century architecture.

The name, variously spelt Olepenne, Ullepenne, is derived from its situation, being on the hill above the Uley. It is rather disappointing that it should have nothing to do with owls, but *three owls argent* appear on the arms of the family of Olepenne, who owned the manor from the early part of the fourteenth century until their heiress brought the property by marriage to John Daunt, who died in 1522. His descendants were still the owners when Rudder wrote in

[1] Rudder's *Gloucestershire*, 1779.

OWLPEN MANOR-HOUSE, GLOUCESTERSHIRE

1779. The entrance gates are evidently much later than the house, and belong to the Queen Anne period.

Shipton Hall, Shropshire, in Corvedale on the road from Much Wenlock to Craven Arms and Ludlow, is a charming example of the latter part of the sixteenth century. It has a tower over the porch, picturesque gables and broad projecting windows. The approach is imposing with its series of terraces and wide stone steps and balustrades. Old-fashioned flowers flourish in the terrace gardens. There is a fine stone dovecot and eighteenth-century stables and outbuildings. The interior shows a noble hall and grand staircase, carved mantelpieces and good panelling. It was formerly the home of the Mytton family, and boasted of a famous collection of old furniture, armour, books, manuscripts, silver, pewter and other family relics ; but all these have vanished, having been sold recently by auction, and the house has passed into the hands of a new owner.

Belonging to the same period is Wilderhope Manor-house in Shropshire. This well-preserved stone-built manor-house, secluded amongst woods and pasture-land, was for many generations the home of the Smallmans. The existing house was either built or largely remodelled by Francis Smallman, who died in 1599. His initials and those of his wife, Ellen, appear on a very beautiful plaster ceiling, together with a half-obliterated legend, of which three at least suggested renderings are given by differing authorities. The mystery of these words together with the high-spirited reputation enjoyed by a certain Major Smallman, of Royalist fame, are probably responsible for strange stories connecting the family and the house with a darkly-spoken-of "Hell-fire Club." The spot is still pointed out, however, where Major Smallman, pursued by enemies, leaped his horse from Wenlock Edge : the horse was killed, but a timely crab-tree broke the major's fall and saved his life.

Wilderhope is now a farmhouse : it has not belonged to

SHIPTON HALL, SHROPSHIRE

the Smallman family since the beginning of the eighteenth century. Its principal front faces south and has three projecting gabled wings, the main entrance being in the eastern projection. It has mullioned windows with Tudor dripstones, and finials at the end of each gable. The many-shafted chimneys are a feature of the house, and there is a curious tower, containing a staircase, with a conical roof somewhat resembling the Scottish type. The part of the house given in the illustration faces north, and shows how well the old builders made allowance for the more exposed side.

Condover Hall is one of the finest of these Shropshire stone houses, built between 1586 and 1598. It is a very perfect example of this period, to which also belong Acton Scott and Upton Cressett; Madeley Court, which also has a cone-shaped roof tower, and Elsich, near Craven Arms, belong to the middle of the sixteenth century, and Benthall and Belswardine to the beginning of that century. The prosperity of the country markedly showed itself in Shropshire during this period, when wealth increased in all ranks, especially among the middle classes, and comfort was more considered than in early days. Squires and merchants, yeomen and tradesmen of every degree, built for themselves houses fitted for the new luxuries, and there is hardly a town or parish in Shropshire that cannot show a house, larger or smaller, of this period.

We have already illustrated (p. 5) Whittington Court, Gloucestershire, a fine house of which some exterior details and interiors are given in a later chapter. The manor of Whittington was granted by Henry VII to the Cottons, and the present house was built by Richard Cotton, who died in 1553, and is commemorated together with his wife in the church near by. Apart from its architecture and the beauty of its surroundings, Whittington Court is of interest as having been the home of Sir John Denham, famed as the author of *Cooper's Hill* and for being Surveyor-General

"WILDERHOPE," SHROPSHIRE

to Charles II. Later the heiress of Whittington brought the main property in marriage to Sir William Morley of Helnaker, and thus it came to Mary, wife of James Earl of Derby, on whose death Helnaker was allowed to fall into ruin. A different fate, however, awaited Whittington, for it was shortly afterwards bought by Thomas Tracy, M.P., who made it his residence, and in 1865 it was very much restored.

On the edge of Salisbury Plain stands the old manor-house of Knook, which has weathered many a storm and is now much dilapidated and liable to fall into decay. The only habitable part is that to the left of the entrance porch, and it is a pity that such a house should become a ruin. It is a good example of a late Tudor house, and is worthy of preservation.

Wiltshire is a county of beautiful old manor-houses. Some of them have fallen from their high estate. Great Chalfield, built in the reign of Henry VI by Thomas Tropenell, in 1460-70, was until recently a ruin, and is now being rescued from its sad condition of neglect. There is a good entrance gate and adjoining it a range of domestic offices. The hall had been made into two storeys, but the dividing floor has been removed. Two curious masks, through the eyes of which the lord could watch the behaviour of his retainers in the hall, have been replaced. Not far away is South Wraxall Manor, a fine stone house, erected by Robert Long, who died in 1447. The portions belonging to that period are the great hall with timber roof of the early hammer-beam type, porch, parlour, kitchens with chamber above and the buttery with withdrawing-room over it. Early in the sixteenth century the gateway with oriel and porter's lodge over it, and the buildings connecting it with the parlour, were erected by Sir Thomas Long, whose badge, the fetterlock, appears over the arch of the gateway. Extensive alterations were carried out in the time of Elizabeth and James I. Some of the fireplaces are very magnificent,

THE OLD MANOR-HOUSE OF KNOOK, WILTS

and are shown in works on architecture. The house was once a school; then it degenerated into a show place where tourists and trippers could have tea-parties. It is now, by the skill and bounty of Mr. E. Richardson Cox, restored to its pristine glories, a model manor-house.

Limestone is the chief building stone of the Isle of Wight which is rich in beautiful specimens of domestic architecture of the humbler sort. Wolverton Manor-house is a good example of the E-shaped plan with its porch and two projecting wings.

As early as the reign of Henry V the manor of Wolverton was owned by the family of Dingley, and in the reign of Elizabeth John Dingley built the present manor-house. The site—surrounded by a moat—of an earlier house can still be traced, but none of the building remains.

Standing on low-lying ground watered by a mill stream, and well equipped with trees, the gabled house, built of warm tinted stone, gives joy to the passer-by. Every side being well broken up there is no monotony in its lines, and from whatever point of view it is seen the effect is good. The entrance front, which faces south-east and is enclosed by the walls of a forecourt, has the projecting wings usual in Isle of Wight houses and also a fine two-storey porch. It is possible that parts of this porch may have once belonged to the earlier house and have been built into the new one.

The south wing has suffered by the insertion of sash windows, and the annexe to the west, designed for a staircase, but used as a brewhouse, is of later date than the house. But on the whole the exterior has been little spoiled or altered. Indeed, the unfinished attics are still in an unplastered condition.

The plan of the interior is much the same as when first designed, and the great hall, which contains a good mantelpiece, has always been kept to its original use.

The mantelpieces in the drawing-room and in one of the

WOLVERTON MANOR-HOUSE, ISLE OF WIGHT

bedrooms were probably added by Sir John Dingley, grandson of the builder, who married Jane Hammond, daughter of Dr. Hammond, Physician-in-Ordinary to Prince Henry, son of James I. Sir John Oglander made a scornful remark of Sir John Dingley, saying that he "lived altogeathor neare London and not in oure Island, as being drawen thethor by ye instigation of his wyfe and her Fryndes."

KINGSTON MANOR, ISLE OF WIGHT

The arms of Hammond impaled with those of Dingley appear carved on a panel in the mantelpiece in the bedroom.

The "pleasance" was doubtless to the north, where the old garden is now.

The old manor-house at Kingston in the island is full of architectural interest, but the modernization of the windows of the south front and the large eighteenth-century chimney-stack, which is a prominent feature of the north front, have done much to deprive it of its original character.

It was built early in the seventeenth century by one of the Meux, a family who had owned the property from the beginning of the fifteenth century. The last baronet, Sir William Meux, died without issue early in the eighteenth century and Kingston passed to his sister. It was about this time that the house suffered a good deal from alteration.

RAM HALL, WARWICKSHIRE

Fortunately, however, the gables still retain their stone copings and their finials (p. 137), similar in detail to those at Barton, and in most instances the lapel moulding to the windows remains. On the upper floor this moulding seems to have been continuous, which suggests the existence formerly of an attic storey, since pulled down or perhaps never finished.

In the present dining-room the Meux arms are carved on a central panel in the elaborate Jacobean chimney-piece, and in the old hall, now used as a kitchen (p. 145), there is a good Jacobean door to the cupboard (p. 163), beside the wide flat-centred chimney-piece. It is panelled as high as the mullioned windows, and has fixed benches attached to the woodwork.

Ram Hall, Warwickshire, stands a memorial of its departed greatness. It has seen better days, but still its twin gables, its mullioned lattice-paned windows, its curiously devised chimney-stack and the half-timbered barn beyond, standing against a bank of giant elms, and the great moat in

EYAM HALL, DERBYSHIRE

front, form a wonderfully charming picture that is not easily forgotten.

There is not much to tell of the history of these houses. They have passed through the ages peacefully and pleasantly. History fails to record any great events that happened in their ancestral halls, or disturbed their placid existence. Plots and conspiracies could not be bred in such quiet homes and if an occasional secret hiding-place tells of dangers feared or actually realized the page of history is silent. They resemble closely their owners, sturdy country squires who hunted and sported, farmed and tried to do their duty to their neighbours, and then slept in the neighbouring churchyard where a simple stone slab records their names and memories.

Not entirely without history, however, is the hall of Eyam. The manor dates back to Saxon times when it was held by one Caschin, and at the Conquest passed into the King's hand. William Peveril became the over-lord in the reign of Henry I, and under him it was held by the Morteynes and then by the Furmivals. Amongst the owners of the manor were the Talbots, earls of Shrewsbury, and the dukes of Devonshire, and the Staffords de Eyham were under-lords of the manor until the family became extinct about a century before the famous Plague that devastated the village. The present manor-house never saw that terrible visitation, which broke out in the year 1665. The old Hall was purchased by the Wright family soon after the Plague, who pulled it down and erected or re-erected it about the year 1680. It is still in the possession of the family and is now the property of Miss Wright. The family is an ancient one, being a branch of the Longstone Wrights who were settled at Longstone Hall in the fourteenth century. The house was evidently constructed on the old lines, and appears to resemble a late Tudor, rather than a building erected at the end of the seventeenth century. It has rough walling with dressed stone at the angles.

There is not much attempt at ornamentation about the houses of Derbyshire and Yorkshire. The stone of which they are constructed is hard and difficult to work. The gable is a general feature, low-pitched and finished with a coping.

Another characteristic north-country house is Cark Hall (given on p. 43), Lancashire. It is a Tudor gabled house with a good Renaissance doorway. You will notice the typical, heavy, north-country chimneys, one of which is circular.

2. TIMBER

We must naturally look for half-timber houses in the great forest districts of the country, in the south-eastern counties, the Weald of Kent and Sussex, Essex and part of Suffolk, in Herefordshire, the Forest of Dean, Shropshire and the Welsh marshes, Lancashire and Cheshire. There we find splendid examples of the skill of the carpenter who fashioned the beautiful timber houses which we so much admire, and which give an added beauty to the English landscape and form a characteristic feature of our scenery. It is impossible to state how early the use of timber for house-construction was invented. It is probable that the Saxons framed their houses of wood and filled in the interstices with "wattle and daub," but most of the existing half-timber buildings date from the fifteenth, sixteenth and seventeenth centuries. Owing to the scarcity of timber few important buildings were erected after that period.

It is unnecessary to describe here the methods adopted for their erection. For information concerning them the reader is referred to Mr. Charles Baily's "Remarks on Timber Houses," published in the *Surrey Archæological Collections*,[1] to Mr. Dawber's Introduction to Mr. W. G. Davies' *Old Cottages in Kent and Sussex*, and to our previous volume on *The Charm of the English Village*. It may be useful, however, to point out the signs which tell of early, or fifteenth-century, work whereby we can distinguish it from the productions of later builders. The older houses have for a corner-post the butt of a tree placed root upwards, with the top part curving diagonally outwards in order to carry the angle-posts of the upper storey. These are often cut into brackets both on the outside and inside of the house. The posts themselves were also richly carved. The closeness of the timbering is one of the characteristics of early

[1] Vol. IV.

work. It was not until later, when timber became scarce, that the timbers were set further apart and curved and shaped braces introduced as shown in the gable illustrated from Bridgnorth. Sometimes the projection of the upper storeys was carried round the angle of the house and continued on all sides. The projecting ends of the joists were rounded off or

TONG

moulded, but it is a sign of early work when they were covered with a long fascia board, either moulded and the upper part cut into small battlements, or carved with foliage. The filling up of the interstices was accomplished in several ways. In some cases upright hazel rods were fixed in grooves cut in the top and bottom of the square panels formed by the upright and horizontal beams, and thinner hazel wands twisted round them. The panel was then filled up with a plaster of clay and chopped straw and

BRIDGNORTH

finished with a coating of lime plaster.[1] Sometimes bricks

[1] R. Nevill, *Old Cottage Architecture in South West Surrey*.

were placed in the divisions between the timbers, and occasionally arranged in herring-bone fashion. Flint and stones in checkered squares are not uncommon in Kent.

Gables also are good indicators of the age of a building, as they are usually adorned with barge-boards. The earliest forms reveal barge-boards with the edges cut in cusps. In the sixteenth century they are pierced with tracery as at Evesham, frequently in the form of trefoils or quatrefoils; and in the Jacobean period the ends of the gables at the eaves have pendants, a finial adorns the ridge, and the perforated designs are more fantastic and correspond to the details of the usual Jacobean carving. In the older houses the barge-boards project about a foot from the surface of the wall. In the eighteenth century, when weather-tiling was introduced, the distance between the wall and the barge-boards was diminished, and ultimately they were placed flush with it; elaborately carved boards were then discarded and the ends of the gable moulded. Other evidences of early or late design will be noticed when we discuss the details of the manor-house.

EVESHAM

The work of building timber-framed houses differed widely in various parts of the kingdom. Thus, owing to the presence of the industrious Flemings, in Eastern England the work in timber, as well as in stone and brick, was more refined than in the remoter regions of the west and north. In Herefordshire, Cheshire and Lancashire the buildings are distinguished by a rude vigour of design and by a coarseness of execution. John Abel, who lived to be ninety-seven years of age, and was born in 1597, was responsible for much good half-timber work in Herefordshire. He built surely and well; his construction was sound and good, but his work was

HUDDINGTON COURT, WORCESTERSHIRE

often a little crude. Mr. Blomfield, in his *History of Renaissance Architecture*, tells of the existence of sundry insidious pattern-books full of atrocious models which were a snare and a delusion to Abel and other carpenter-builders, and led them away from their truer instincts and traditional styles. New fashions ill understood did not go well with the lingering spirit of Gothic architecture or the scarcely acquired conceptions of the Renaissance. After this time a traditional vernacular method of working again arose in England. The local builders, masons and carpenters, recovered their lost art and worked in their own natural and true style; and we find "in the seventeenth and eighteenth centuries the independence of thought, the sober taste and kindliness of manner which has throughout stamped our architecture, whether Mediæval or Renaissance, with a character unmistakably English."[1]

Herefordshire is famous for its timber houses. Weobley still retains a large number of beautiful old black and white structures, which were universal in the county two hundred years ago. In the county we find Knill Court, which was enlarged about 1561; Orleton Court, the seat of the Blount family; the Wythall, near Ross; the Ley in Weobley, the residence of the family of Brydges, and built by James Brydges in 1589, with no fewer than eight gables on the north front; Luntley Court in Dilwyn, dated 1674.

We will work up these western shires and notice the types of timber-framed houses which abound there. Huddington Court is an old moated manor-house in the heart of rural Worcestershire, not far from Droitwich. The romance of history is woven round this old half-timbered house, with its encircling moat, aged walls and twisted chimney. It is celebrated as the place where the conspirators of the Gunpowder Plot halted during their last melancholy fight after the plot had been discovered and they knew that they were

[1] *Renaissance Architecture in England*, by R. Blomfield.

SOLIHULL, WARWICKSHIRE

doomed if captured. It was the home of the Wintours of Hodington, one Joan de Hodington marrying Roger Wintour, a descendant of Wyntour the Castellan of Carnarvon. Robert Wyntour, the conspirator, came of an ancient and powerful Roman Catholic family. He married Gertrude Talbot of Grafton, the daughter of the wealthiest landholder in the county. But his restless spirit, his religious fanaticism made him the victim of the mad visionaries and traitors who devised the Gunpowder Plot. On November 6th, 1605, a weary company of exhausted and dejected travel-stained men rode across the bridge to Huddington Court. In the east window of the Court (still called Lady Wyntour's window) sat Robert Wyntour's wife watching for the return of her husband. Robert's brothers, Thomas and John, were also involved, and here in this hall they met, for the last time, fugitives from justice, well knowing the fate that awaited them. The dining-hall is now divided, by a lath-and-plaster partition, into two bedrooms, but the fine stone chimney-piece remains, with the arms of Huddington and Cromby and the royal arms of Edward III. The company on that memorable night numbered thirty, including Catesby, Percy, Rookwood and Sir Everard Digby. Guards watched at the corners of the roads. At 3 a.m. the weary men rose from sleep to attend Mass. Arms and ammunition and armour were laid out in the hall for their use, and a few hours later the conspirators were in the saddle again, and Robert Wyntour had embraced his wife and children for the last time and bid farewell for ever to the home of his ancestors.

The neighbouring county of Warwick has several notable houses, and amongst these is the curious half-timbered mansion known as Bott's Green House, near Shustoke, to which we have already referred (p. 7).

In the same county is the house at Solihull, reputed to be the original manor-house of the Greswoldes, distinguished by its two oriel windows jutting out in the central bay. Sash windows have been inserted in the ground floor.

The coloured frontispiece to this volume shows Grimshaw Hall, in Warwickshire, a delightful timber and plaster house with projecting porch, shallow bay windows supported by brackets and brick clustered chimneys.

HARTON MANOR-HOUSE, SHROPSHIRE

Shropshire is famous for its black and white houses, notably the old town of Shrewsbury where they abound. Pitchford Hall dates back to 1475, and the house on the Wyle Cop, where Henry of Richmond slept in 1485, still stands to show how well men built in the fifteenth century. Park Hall is a magnificent example of a half-timbered front of 1555, and Marrington Hall of 1595. At Durvall there is a fine timber house of about 1580. Boscobel, well known for its associations with Charles II, was built at the close of the sixteenth century, or at the very beginning of the seventeenth, and Plowden Hall is of about the same date. In both of these houses you will find some ingeniously devised hiding-places or priests' holes. When in these difficult days we manage to save any money we take it to the bank. In Elizabethan times there were no banks and few opportunities for investing money. Hence our forefathers kept their money in their houses and cleverly devised secret cupboards and hiding-holes, where they could deposit their superfluous wealth. It is surprising how many nooks and corners and secret holes you can find in an old-fashioned escritoire. The little Harton Manor-house embowered in trees is a good example of the smaller type. The ornamented curved braces in the gable are peculiar, showing some attempt at elaborate decoration, and the clustered chimney-stack displays fine workmanship. The view we give of the Great Lyth in the same county (p. 103) shows a fine brick house with curved gables.

Crossing the boundary into the neighbouring county of Stafford, we admire the half-timbered Bradley Hall at Kingswinford, which conforms to the usual type of the Midland manor-house. It bears the date 1596, and we notice chimneys wide at the base so as to afford a pleasantly large inglenook which is probably combined with an oven, the closeness of the upright timbers, the overhanging of the storeys so that the front of the gable embraces the large bay window and the ingeniously constructed porch which is carried up to the roof and has rooms over it.

Cheshire has many houses of the black and white type as well as of the red sandstone which mellows so beautifully with age and seems part of the scenery. Of the former Handforth Hall is a delightful example. It is rich in beauty and in romance. The Honfords of Honford (such is the old

BRADLEY HALL, KINGSWINFORD, STAFFORDSHIRE

spelling of the name) were a sturdy race, like many of the other old families of Cheshire :—

> Strong in the arm
> And weak in head.

One fought in the Crusades and took for his cognizance a wondrous star that fell from heaven before the armies of Saladin. Another fought in France against Jeanne d'Arc, and the last of the heirs-male fell fighting against the Scots at Cheviot Moor. He left a daughter Margaret, who married first Sir John Stanley, the warrior sung by Sir Walter Scott, who quarrelled with the Leghs and became a monk, and secondly Uryan Brereton who built the present hall, as the inscription over the door testifies :—

> This haulle was buylded In the yeare of oure Lord God M.CCCCC.LXII. by Uryan Breretoun Knight whom maryed Margaret daughter and heyre of Wyllyam Handforth of Handforthe Esquyer & had Issue vi sonnes and ii daughters.

The Breretons played a manly part in the history of the shire, but the glories of the old house have departed. It is only a farmhouse now, and not long ago its poor furniture was sold by auction. But Uryan Brereton built surely and well, and the grand old staircase and panelling bear witness to his skill and a hiding-hole in the stairs to his ingenuity.

In the neighbouring county of Lancashire can be seen many good houses of stone or brick according to the nature of the land, but some of the "magpie" houses are the most highly finished and carefully wrought. As an example we give the interesting Hall i' th' Wood at Tonge, a good specimen of late sixteenth-century half-timber work with a stonework addition. Hall i' th' Wood is a charming house, very peaceful and dignified as it looks down upon the busy bustling Bolton town with reeking chimneys and noisy factories. In the quaint Lancashire tongue it tells by its

HANDFORTH HALL, CHESHIRE

name that it was once girt with tall trees, but these have nearly all vanished. The initials "$L^{B}B$" over a fireplace with the date 1591 declare its builder to have been Laurence Brownlowe of Tonge, grandson of Roger, who held lands here in 1499. Half a century later a daughter brought the property by marriage to Alexander Norris, who built the

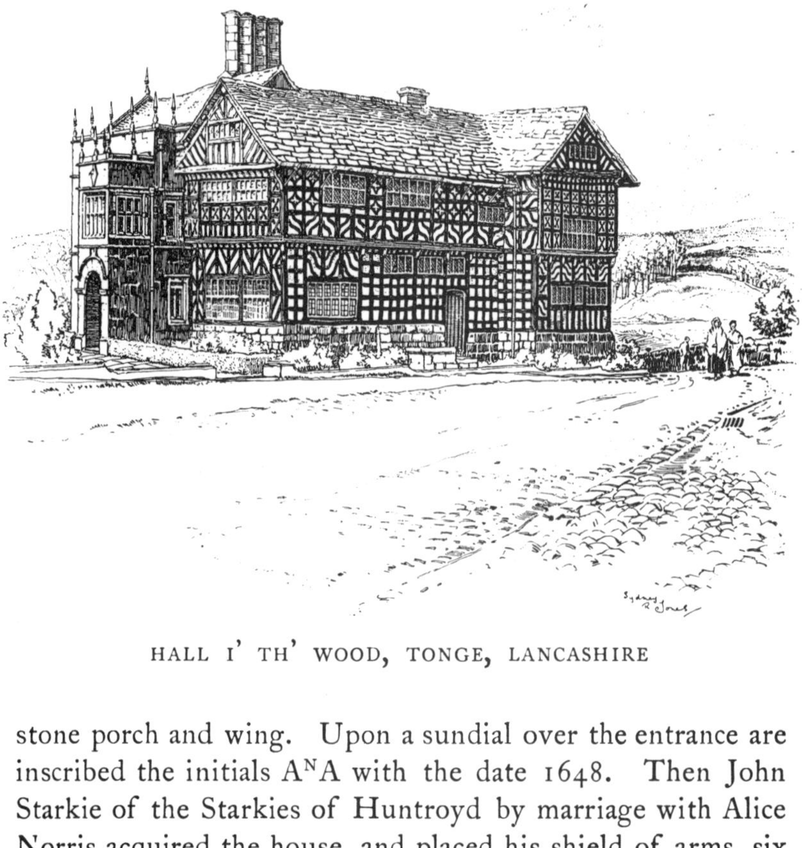

HALL I' TH' WOOD, TONGE, LANCASHIRE

stone porch and wing. Upon a sundial over the entrance are inscribed the initials $A^{N}A$ with the date 1648. Then John Starkie of the Starkies of Huntroyd by marriage with Alice Norris acquired the house, and placed his shield of arms, six stalks, in the hall. The house fell upon evil days. Poor Samuel Crompton, the inventor of the spinning jenny, lived here and worked and starved. The Starkies lived on their estates at Huntroyd, and the old house became a ruin. It has been carefully restored and is now a museum, having been

"ST. MARY'S," BRAMBER, SUSSEX

purchased by Mr. Lever and presented to the Bolton Corporation. You enter the house through the stone porch erected in 1648. There is a grand oak door with long flowery-ended hinges and studded with nails. A fine staircase leads to the withdrawing-room. The windows are lofty with mullions and transoms. There is a good plaster ceiling in three compartments, and a seventeenth-century mantelpiece with pilasters and caryatides. Some of the details of the panelling and other features will be noticed later on.

Journeying to the south-eastern district we find some excellently finished work of the carpenter's craft, which was indeed an art. "Some of these old buildings are works of art, that is, they show that intangible quality, the result of growth and life, which no artificial rules or mechanical means can achieve; those employed on the building were doing creative work, according to their capacity, for their fellows, who were competent to appreciate success or failure."[1] In Surrey and Sussex the local materials are numerous. We find walls of stone and brick, half timber and plaster, half timber and tile-hanging. Red brick sometimes fills the panels of half-timbered walls, and the roofs are of thatch or Horsham slabs or tiles. Great Tangley Manor-house is a good example of a Surrey house. We can trace the old plan, the great hall with screens and entrances, and the insertion of the upper floor at the end of the sixteenth century when the present front was added.

We give an illustration of the charming house called St. Mary's, Bramber, Sussex, as an example of an early timber-framed house. It is part of the manor of Bidlington, distinct from Bramber, and was originally a small hospital dedicated to St. Mary Magdalene, in charge of a prioress. At its dissolution it became the property of Magdalen College, Oxford, and was leased by the college to the Lid-

[1] *Old Cottages and Farm-houses in Surrey*, by W. Curtis Green. Illustrated by W. Galsworthy Davie.

BROAD STREET, KENT

bettor family who held it for three centuries.[1] In such houses as these we do not find the same general character and appearance which we noticed in the buildings of Lancashire, Cheshire and Shropshire. These lack the elaborate setting-out of panels with diapering and cusping, and as a rule we find only the plain vertical timbering varied sometimes by the curved braces.[2] A very fine Kentish house is that at Broad Street with its picturesque gable of the fifteenth century, the edges being foliated. The little battlemented facia that runs over the edges of the joists, the latticed windows and square-leaded panes, and long stretch of tiled roofing, are all distinctive features. A larger and more important house is St. Benedict's Priory, near Tenterden, already given (p. 41), a region renowned for its pleasant houses full of quiet charm and repose. It would be hard to devise a more picturesque grouping of the roofs and gables, of bays and oriel with curved supporting bracket.

It often happens that the timbers of a half-timbered house in course of ages shrink and the wattle and daub panels become less impervious to the weather. Hence our forefathers were compelled to adopt other means to keep themselves warm, to keep out the draughts and the rain. Sometimes they hung the outside walls with tiles, or covered them with weather-boarding, or plastered them over. Behind these layers of tiles, or boards, or plaster, the old half-timbered house still remains. Such a tile-hung half-timbered structure is Old Shoyswell, in Sussex, in the northern part of the parish of Etchingham, not far from Ticehurst. It dates from the early part of the sixteenth century, and is a very good example of the half-timber work of its period and county. Tradition states that it was a hunting-lodge of King Henry VIII, but the history of the manor is opposed to this theory, as during his reign and for a long period

[1] *History of the Castles, Mansions and Manors of Western Sussex*, by Elwes (1876).

[2] *Old Cottages and Farm-houses in Kent and Sussex*, by E. Guy Dawber.

it was held by a family who took their name from the place.

Judging from the few facts of their history that it is possible to glean, the Shoyswells must have been a rather delightful family. They owned the property of Shoyswell from about the middle of the thirteenth until the end of the seventeenth century, when the family became extinct. It is likely that a certain Elizabeth Shoyswell was the wife

OLD SHOYSWELL, SUSSEX

of William de Etchingham, the rebuilder of Etchingham Church, as the Shoyswell arms, "three horseshoes of the field," appear impaled with those of Etchingham, on the brass which commemorates him.

Thomas Shoyswell in his will dated 1580 makes some crisp bequests to his wife Dorothy, amongst them being "the use and weringe of her weddinge ringe during her lief" and "free liberty to bake and brewe in the bakehouse and brewhouse for her owne necessarie use and to drye her clothes uppon the hedges and bushes about his mannor-house of Shoyswell." She is also to have the "Chamber in his howse called the Grene Chamber, and the Chamber within the same, together with free ingress, egresse and regresse into and from the same by the ways, droves, and stayers used and accustomed to the same (together with wood for fuel) and the garret over the Greene Chamber."

This domestic autocrat was probably the builder of the present house, and on account of his skill in rearing this pleasant dwelling-place perhaps his tyranny may be forgiven him.

3. BRICK

It is usually supposed that the use and knowledge of brick-work disappeared with the departure of the Romans and were not rediscovered until the thirteenth century, when Little Wenham Hall arose in Suffolk about the year 1260 A.D. It is suggested that the making of bricks was not a lost art during these several centuries, that the old name for a brick was tigel or tile, and that these thin tile-like bricks were made in England both in Saxon and Norman times. But the old tradition is doubtless correct, and we may assume that whatever bricks were used prior to the thirteenth century were the old Roman bricks taken from disused villas or abandoned walls. Their reintroduction was due to the industrious Flemings who migrated into East Anglia and brought with them the art which they had long practised in their own country, where there is a complete absence of building stone. Probably they brought their bricks with them, and it is supposed that those which were used for Little Wenham Hall were imported. A good description of this house is given in Turner and Parker's *Domestic Architecture* :—

"The plan is a parallelogram, with a square tower at one angle : on the outside the scroll moulding is used as a string, and it is continued all round, showing that the house now is entire as originally built : at one angle, where the external staircase was originally placed, some other building seems to have been added at a later period, though since removed : of this additional structure an Elizabethan doorway remains, with an inscription built in above it. The ground floor is vaulted with a groined vault of brick, with stone ribs which are merely chamfered; they are carried on semi-octagon shafts with plainly moulded capitals. The windows of this lower room are small plain lancets, widely splayed internally.

"The upper room has a plain timber roof, and the fire-place is blocked up. The windows have seats in them; and at the end of the room near the door is a recess or niche

LITTLE WENHAM HALL, SUFFOLK

forming a sort of cupboard. Both house and tower are covered with flat leaden roofs, having brick battlements all round, with a coping formed of moulded bricks or tiles, some of which are original, and others of the Elizabethan period. The tower is a story higher than the body of the house, and has a similar battlement and coping: the crenelles, which are at rather long intervals, are narrow, with wide merlons between them. In one corner of the tower is a turret with a newel staircase.

"On the upper story of the projecting square tower is a chapel, which opens into the large room or hall at one corner.

It is a small vaulted chamber : the east window is of three lights, with three foliated circles in the head, of early English character : the north and south windows are small lancets widely splayed within : in the east jamb of the south window is a very good piscina, with a detached shaft at the angle, the capital of which has good early English mouldings : the basin is destroyed. On the north side of the altar-piece is another niche, like a piscina, but without any basin : it has a trefoil head and a bold scroll moulding for a hood terminated by masks. The vault is of a single bay, with good ribs, of early English character, springing from corbels, the two eastern being heads, the two western plain tongues."

The builders of this old hall evidently strove after domestic comfort as well as to provide some defence against an enemy. The times were not then ripe for the abandonment of fortifications. Though bricks were used so extensively in this Suffolk house, they did not become a common building material for some time. In the fifteenth century we find many notable houses built of brick, such as Tattershall Castle, Lincolnshire ; the old Palace, Hatfield (now the stables) ; Oxburgh Hall, Norfolk ; Hurstmonceaux Castle, Sussex ; and Layer Marney, Essex. Wherever the Flemings settled, there we find the early use of brick. In East Kent they left their traces, in such places as Rye and Sandwich, until at length by the time Elizabeth came to the throne brickwork had become common. Many great houses were constructed of this material, and the country squires began to use it for their manor-houses. An important Flemish feature introduced were the crow-steps or corbie-steps along the gables of houses. The bricks used were much thinner than those used now, and varied from 1½ inches to 2 inches in thickness. Between each course was a thick layer of mortar, and this arrangement of thin bricks and thick mortar is one of the causes of the picturesqueness of these old houses, which far surpass in beauty our modern erections of thick, machine-made bricks with little mortar.

Wormleighton Manor-house, in Warwickshire, is a very fine example of late Henry VIII style. The bay was originally carried up to the second storey;[1] otherwise the building seems practically unaltered. It is the property of Earl Spencer, and is honoured by bibliophiles as being the house where the Spencer Library was formed. The Spencers of Wormleighton, like many of their neighbours, made a

WORMLEIGHTON MANOR-HOUSE, WARWICKSHIRE

great fortune in the wool trade and reared this house. The manor belonged to the Earl of Mellent at the Conquest, was afterwards owned by the De Clintons, and was acquired by the Spencers in 1506. Lawrence Washington and his sons, Sir William and Sir John, were frequent guests at the old house, and also at Althorp. During the Civil War it was garrisoned for the King, and then abandoned. Prince Rupert slept here the night before the Edgehill fight. The interior

[1] An old print of the house shows the continuation of the bay.

shows the remains of the "star chamber," the clock tower and the Tudor hall.

In the original home of brickwork, in East Anglia, we may expect to find some of the most perfect examples of brick buildings, and Parham Old Hall, the home of the Willoughbys, now the property of Mr. H. C. Corrance, presents one of the most picturesque. It was never a very great house, and is now a somewhat decayed farmhouse. It rises sheer out of its broad tree-girt moat, its walls of rich red where the bricks are crumbling, of green and grey and yellow where they are overspread with moss and lichens. It was built by Sir Christopher de Parham, father of the first Lord Willoughby de Parham, between the years 1498 and 1527. The manor came to the family through the marriage of Lord Willoughby d'Eresby with a daughter of the Earl of Suffolk in the time of Edward III. You can trace a resemblance between the bay windows and chimney-shafts of this beautiful old house with the better-preserved work at East Barsham, Great Snoring, Oxburgh and Cressingham. You cross the bridged moat under a gateway bearing five coats-of-arms and admire the building which a long period of neglect and decay, the roughly repaired windows and roofs, cannot rob of its beauty. George Crabbe, the poet, lived here, having loved and won Sarah Elmy, the niece of John Tovell, a yeoman farmer, who resided at Parham Hall. Crabbe's son and biographer thus describes the house :—

"His house was large, and the surrounding moat, the rookery, the ancient dovecot and the well-stored fish-ponds were such as might have suited a gentleman's seat of some consequence, but one side of the house immediately overlooked a farmyard full of all sorts of domestic animals and the scene of constant bustle and noise. On entering the house there was nothing at first sight to remind one of the farm—a spacious hall, paved with black and white marble ; at one extremity a very handsome drawing-room, and at the other a fine old staircase of black oak, polished till it was as

PARHAM OLD HALL, SUFFOLK

slippery as ice, and having a chime-clock and a barrel-organ on its landing-places. But this drawing-room, a corresponding dining parlour, and a handsome sleeping apartment upstairs were all *tabooed* ground, and made use of on great and solemn occasions only."

The house has shrunk somewhat since then, and has lost some of its ancient features. It is a pity that no friendly hand can be outstretched to restore it to its former greatness.

Another old Norfolk house is Barnham Broom, a fine specimen of old brickwork. The manor was held of Castle-Acre Castle, and came to the Mortimers, in whose family it remained for some time, and then passed by marriage to the Chamberlains, who held it during the sixteenth and seventeenth centuries; it was then sold to Sir Thomas Woodhouse of Kimberley, and is now owned by the Earl of Kimberley. It is a long building under a span roof with an important porch three storeys high projecting into the garden. The crow-stepped gables and fine chimney-stacks, its walls pierced with windows of all shapes and sizes and in all kinds of odd positions, are worthy of notice. The door and window mouldings, which at first sight appear to be of stone, are really brick plastered over. The square pieces running up either side of the gable are also thin layers of plaster. This practice of covering brick with plaster is fairly common in Norfolk. The house retains many of the features of the hall with screens. Now a long corridor runs the whole length of the house. The old hall has been divided, but the bay window indicates its former size. There is an upstairs room with a fine plaster ceiling bearing the date 1614. A door is illustrated on p. 126.

Kirstead Old Hall, the property of Viscount Canterbury, now used as a farmhouse, is a very picturesque old manor-house. It preserves the tradition of the hall with porch and two wings. The red brickwork and tiles display brilliant colouring. A pleasing effect is produced by the diaper

THE OLD HALL, BARNHAM BROOM, NORFOLK

lozenge-shaped pattern formed by the insertion of black-headed bricks. The crow-stepped gables are again seen here. The windows are mullioned with pedimented heads, and the number of lights decreases as they approach the summit of the gable. The date 1614 is inscribed over the pedimented entrance doorway.

In East Kent Flemish influence was strong, but the builders of brickwork dwellings belonged to a different school from that which swayed the ideas of the East Anglian artificers. As an example of late sixteenth-century house we give an illustration of Sturry Court, the seat of Lord Milner. It is a good instance of the East Kent type. We notice the imposing gateway flanked by heavy buttresses, and encircling wall with sunk bays, the object of which seems to have been purely decorative. The manor of Sturry formed one of the original possessions of St. Augustine's Monastery at Canterbury, and it was at Sturry that the abbots had their summer residence. Indeed, the last abbot, who, after the dissolution of the abbey, was sole owner of the manor, died at Sturry. The present building, however, which dates from 1583, was the property and residence of the Lords Strangford. Later it suffered a fate common to many sixteenth-century manor-houses and descended to the level of a farmhouse, but in 1905 it was restored by Viscount Milner, and is once more the dwelling of a nobleman.

Foreign influence is again seen in the gables formed of combinations of curves. These came into fashion at a period later than the crow-stepped gables, many of the houses which have this characteristic bearing dates from the middle to the end of the seventeenth century.

The house at Littlebourne in East Kent and one at Sarre give examples of these, and furnish us with instances of the ingenious method in which a blank wall can be treated and a gable decorated by the simple use of tile and brick. Courses of brick intermingled with occasional courses of tiles ingeni-

KIRSTEAD OLD HALL, NORFOLK

STURRY COURT, EAST KENT

ously arranged with curves and slopes, and in the centre of the gable an elliptical bit of plaster in a curved frame of brick, add diversity to the whole scheme and give an attrac-

AT LITTLEBOURNE, EAST KENT

tive appearance. The effect is produced simply with the aid of plain unmoulded bricks. The chimneys of these Kentish houses form a very important feature. They are ingeniously contrived with various projections and settings forward, showing a love of novelty and of change on the part of their designers. But these we shall consider in detail in a later chapter.

The same love of diversity is shown in other examples of brickwork, notably in the details of the brickwork at Sarre. The string courses that extend around the house and the

SARRE LITTLEBOURNE

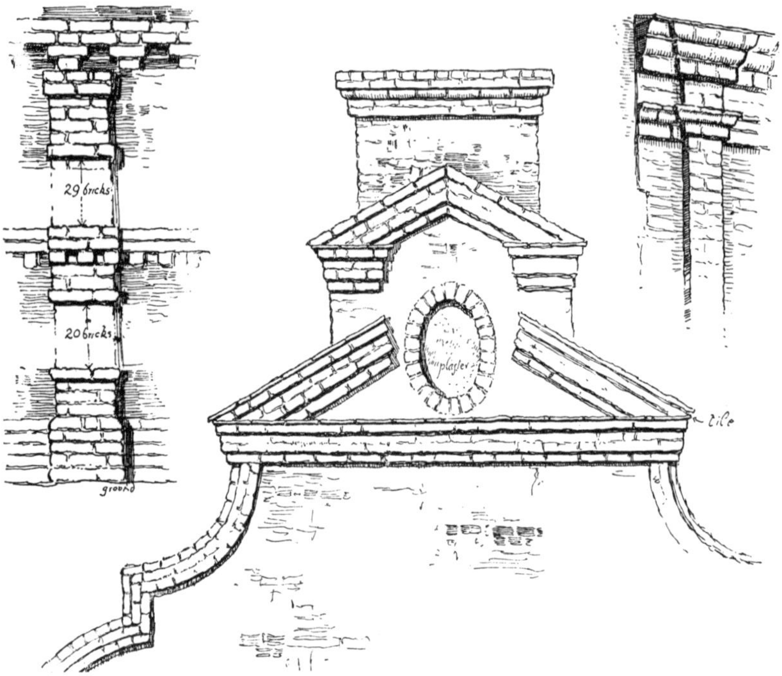

BRICK DETAILS FROM EAST KENT

pilasters on the surface of the wall are quaintly devised and admirably executed.

Wandering away westward we come to Leicestershire, and find an interesting piece of brickwork mingled with stone in the manor-house known as Groby Old Hall, where the court leet and court baron are still held, a reminiscence of its former dignity. The wall between the two towers is an addition, and also the buildings on the right of the illustration. The house, now much dilapidated, was once the home of the Barons Ferrers of Groby, and is renowned in history, as here Elizabeth Woodville, afterwards the queen of Edward IV, lived happily as the wife of Sir John Grey. On his death, at the battle of St. Albans in 1461, the estate was forfeited and passed into the hands of the King.

We give two views of the Herefordshire brick and timber house known as Nunupton Court. It is unfortunately unin-

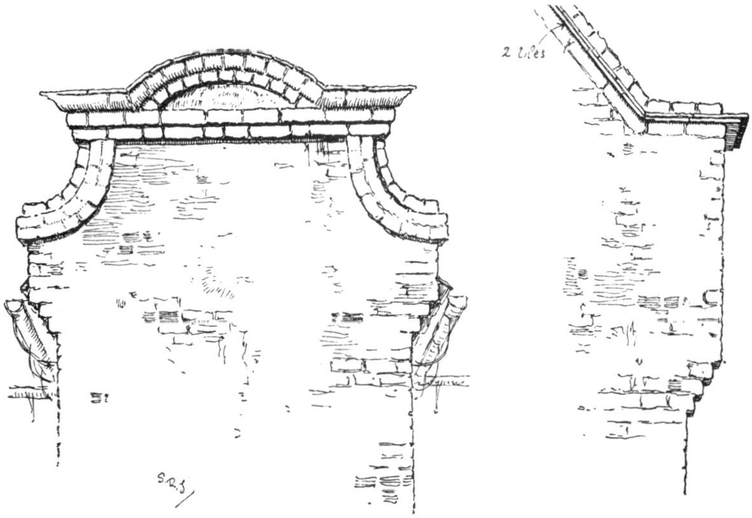

LITTLEBOURNE

BRICK DETAILS FROM EAST KENT

habited and fast falling into decay. It is sad that such a picturesque pile should be doomed, and the attention of the National Trust for the Preservation of Places of Historic Interest and of the Society for the Protection of Ancient Buildings should be called to its forlorn condition. The timber porch, roofed with slabs, with its carved bargeboards, the graceful gables shaped with segments of circles and finials, the fine chimney-stacks, one of which is a triumph of the bricklayer's art of the seventeenth century, the encircling wall of the terrace, all combine to form a

THE OLD HALL, GROBY, LEICESTERSHIRE

picture of great beauty, and show that the skill of the bricklayers in Herefordshire was no less than that of the

NUNUPTON COURT, HEREFORDSHIRE

carpenter-builder who reared such fine half-timbered dwellings in this western county.

The illustration of the Great Lyth shows a quaint old

brick house in a country more frequently associated with timber building. There is, however, some good work in brick to be met with, as at the Crow Leasow, near Ludlow. The Great Lyth stands on the sharp slope of Lyth Hill, near the Shropshire mining district. Within a few miles are Condover Hall, a fine sandstone house already mentioned, and the enormous half-timber Hall at Pitchford, good instances of the variety of Shropshire building materials.

NUNUPTON COURT, HEREFORDSHIRE

Our last illustration of brickwork is a view of the manor-house at Penn in Buckinghamshire, which with several other eighteenth-century houses forms the modern part of this old-world village. The manor belonged to the family of Penn late in the fifteenth century, and remained theirs until the death of Roger Penn in 1732, when it passed through marriage with the heiress to Sir Nathaniel Curzon.

THE GREAT LYTH, LYTH HILL, NEAR SHREWSBURY, SALOP

PENN, BUCKINGHAMSHIRE

4. FLINT

Where chalk abounds there many flints are discovered which form such a useful and pleasing material for building. In the south-eastern counties of England, in Kent, Surrey, Sussex, Wilts and Berkshire, Hampshire, Dorset, Isle of Wight, East Anglia, you will find many houses constructed of flint, or of flint combined with other materials such as brick or plaster. In Norfolk it was a common custom to build walls of black and white flints, the external angles of the dwelling and the quoins of the doors and windows being of brick. On the Isle of Thanet and the east coast of Kent a similar method of building was employed. In this region a local variety of treatment is observable. The main walling is of flint marked by occasional bonding courses of brickwork which are often treated in a peculiar and picturesque manner. Patterns of diaper in brick are sometimes

STOCKTON MANOR-HOUSE, WILTSHIRE

used to enliven the flintwork, or a pattern in flints relieves the monotony of the brickwork. In Wiltshire we find stone and flint combined, as in the case of Longford Castle, begun in 1580, where the wall face of the towers "is divided into oblong panels by bands of white stone and black flints alternately."[1] Stockton Manor is a good stone and flint house with Elizabethan gables. The stone and flint run in alternate courses, giving a most pleasing effect.

The beautiful moated mansion of Elsing Hall, Norfolk, rebuilt about 1470 by Sir John Hastings, presents many interesting features with its two projecting gables, the upper parts being constructed of half-timber work. All the walls are of flint with stone dressings. Sustead Old Hall, once the manor-house of the Wyndhams, which bears on its gables the date 1663, has its main walls constructed of squared and faced flints with brick angles and dressings to the windows. Great freedom is often used. At Shapwick we find stone, brick and flint introduced into cob-walling.

5. PLASTER

In the construction of timber-framed houses we noticed the use of wattle and daub for the filling up of the panels formed by the horizontal and vertical timbers. The builders of our old houses were not content to leave the surface plain and unadorned. The panels pleaded for decoration and did not cry in vain. In many cases the whole of the surface of the walls was plastered over, and this afforded a wide field for the plasterer's art, and he did not fail to make extensive use of it. His art was called Pargeting or Parge-work. His material was simple, ordinary lime and sand and hair, mixed with some cow-dung and road scrapings. Now his art has almost died out. Professor Lethaby tells that in the eastern and southern counties "by careful inquiry you may find an old workman who remembers seeing it done when

[1] *Renaissance Architecture in England*, by R. Blomfield.

he was young, who can describe the tools and knows the patterns—'tortoise-shell,' 'square-picking,' and the rest." The village plasterer had his own patterns which he varied with skill. His neighbouring rival worked out his own devices ; so there is often much variation. In Essex you will find the zigzag incised on the plaster, the whole surface

CROWN HOUSE, NEWPORT, ESSEX

being pricked with a pointed stick. Sometimes a fan of pointed sticks was used. Some patterns were scalloped, and some done in wavy or flowing lines, and others with thin wavy lines intersected or interlaced like basket-work.

The artist sometimes strove after great inventions and produced curious figures of men or birds or animals, but these usually turned out to be unconsciously designed grotesques or burlesques. Sometimes he would simply cut patterns through the top layer of the plaster down to the coating beneath, but he was an ingenious person and discovered

THE PORCH, CROWN HOUSE, NEWPORT, ESSEX

a far better plan. He cut out thin pieces of wood into the shape of desired pattern and arranged these in borders and panels and then "rough casted" round them up to the level of these inserted pieces. Then he removed the pieces of wood, and lo! there were left charming little recessed patterns which he emphasized by colouring them with apple-greens, ochre-yellows and earthy reds.[1] The scrollwork, shells, figures, foliage and other devices were all moulded by hand and with the tools of the craftsman, and often bear witness to his artistic skill, though his figures were not examples of perfect modelling. Later on moulds were used.

We give an interesting example of external parge-work in the house at Newport called the Crown House, which tradition says was inhabited by the fascinating Nell Gwyn, who died in 1687. The date 1692, which appears on the house, probably refers to its restoration and to the erection of the porch. The plaster-work is excellent, but it is being sadly worn by the severity of the English climate. Between the windows on each floor is a panel formed by mouldings of simple section. The modelling in those on the first floor is of some sort of plant springing out of small vessels. Horizontal panels are grouped on each side of the central doorway, under the middle first-floor windows, with slight enrichments therein. A kind of label runs over the top of the ground-floor window heads with a dotted pattern above and below. The lower panels are quite plain, but have an inner panelled surface of plain plaster. The shell porch is a very attractive feature, and in the panel over it a crown appears. The house remains as a very good example of the plasterer's art.

We shall refer to interior plaster-work in a subsequent chapter. For the exterior of buildings decorative plaster-work did not survive the seventeenth century, and owing to

[1] *The Art of the Plasterer*, by G. P. Bankart.

THE MANOR HOUSE, CAVENDISH, SUFFOLK

BALLINGDON OLD HALL, ESSEX

the severity of our climate and the destruction of old houses not many examples are left. Wyvenhoe, near Colchester, has a very fine example of parge-work covering the whole front of the house above the ground floor. The plasterer did not approve of his work being injured by village urchins or wanton destroyers, so he usually confined his works of art to the upper storeys where they were well out of the reach of foolish and mischievous folk. At Saffron Walden on a house there are some rather weird birds and foliage. Sparrow's House, Ipswich, has some elaborate but rather childish representations of Europe, Asia and Africa, with scrolled leafage and masks, fruit and leaves, birds and flowers, and Neptune riding a sea-horse, a swan and hunting scene. We can find several other examples in Maidstone, York, Canterbury, Earl's Colne (Colneford House) and in several other places, but as these are principally in towns or on the walls of homely cottages they scarcely come within the compass of this book.

Many beautiful manor-houses are constructed of timber and wholly plastered over. Such is the sixteenth-century manor-house of Cavendish, Suffolk, reputed to have been one of the early homes of the Devonshire family. Inside the house there are two plaster escutcheons of the Cavendish arms. The house has now been converted into a village club. Another fine manor-house is Ballingdon Old Hall, near Sudbury, Essex.

We give an illustration of an excellent example of parge-work which can be seen in the picturesque village of Steventon in Berkshire. In few parts of England can you find more delightful bits of half-timbered domestic architecture of the fifteenth, sixteenth and seventeenth centuries than in this secluded village. Primitive porches, antique roofs and gables, latticed windows and ancient doorways abound, showing the abundance of oak trees that once grew in the district, and proclaiming the dexterity of the village craftsmen. Inside,

AT STEVENTON, BERKSHIRE

many of the houses are panelled in oak, with massive oak tie-beams, quaint old staircases, solid flooring and original roofs, as sound as when they were constructed three centuries ago. We give an illustration of one of the most remarkable of the old houses, dated 1657, with its pargeted front, its graceful bay and oriel windows, its barge-boards, while within are two curiously panelled and painted rooms. The pavement in front is part of the old "Causey" or causeway, or flood-path, extending the whole length of the village street and planted with trees on both sides. Tradition states that it was constructed by the monks who dwelt at the small priory in the village, a cell of the abbey of Hellouin, in Normandy, but an inscription in the church on a dole-board tells that "Two sisters by ancient report gave a yard land one acre of meadow four swathes one Taylers yeard one close and a copps to ye maintenance of ye Causeway of Steventon." This inscription puzzles the learned, and no one quite knows what it means; but at any rate the gift of the two sisters yields £30 a year, which serves to keep the causeway in repair and for lighting it during winter. The plaster-work on this old house is simple and effective, and is not unworthy to appear as an illustration of the kind of decoration which our forefathers loved to bestow upon their manor-houses and on other less ambitious dwellings in the village community.

V

EXTERIOR DETAILS

WE now pass on to admire the architectural details of the manor-houses of England. Their plans, the general views of their beautiful exteriors, their harmony with their setting amidst the shade of tall trees, or amidst the rugged hills of Derbyshire or Yorkshire, the variety of the materials of their construction, the skill and care of their builders, have all been noticed ; but it remains to examine the means whereby our forefathers obtained these good effects and admire the loving attention bestowed upon the picturesque details which made their homes so fair and beautiful. A man may produce fairly good work in many walks of life, and yet not attain to success, because he lacks the ability and application to master the details of his profession, and can never rise above the common-place. It is so in architecture. We will, therefore, endeavour to learn the secrets of the beauties of these old buildings, cultivate the spirit which produced them and understand the surpassing merits of their details.

First and most striking among the exterior details are

I. CHIMNEYS

The oldest houses had no chimneys. The fire burned in the centre of the hall and the smoke floated like a cloud over the heads of the guests and then made its escape through the louvre. Fireplaces with chimneys were first constructed in the solars and private family apartments of the house, and then in the fifteenth century they began to appear on one side of the hall, nearer to the dais than to the screens, and when the dog-grate was filled with burning logs it looked fairly comfortable, imparted some heat into the room and made it a little less chilly. The chimneys as they grew followed the architectural style of the period in which they were constructed, being Decorated or Perpendicular, and the Gothic style and tradition are still discernible in the chimney when the workmen were busy devising new inventions. In the Cotswolds we find specially fine examples of chimneys, which are the most characteristic features of the houses in that district of good masonry, and the old Gothic treatment is clearly seen in houses at Burford, Kingham, Bredon, Bibury and elsewhere. We give an illustration of the chimney at Harringworth, which is early and retains all its Gothic details. These chimneys have usually octagonal or circular shafts pierced with lancet openings and crowned at the top with a pyramidal roof. Another example is shown in the old manor-house at Preston (p. 21). Sometimes the chimney-stack appears in the centre of the ridge, at others

HARRINGWORTH

SANDFORD ORCAS

SANDFORD ORCAS

on the apex of the gables, as at Sandford Orcas, a fine bold octagonal stack enriched at the top by Gothic carving. In the same manor-house there is the other chimney, oblong in section, the cap of which is treated as a cornice enriched with spiral ornament of Gothic design and lower down adorned with mouldings. Sometimes the early chimneys are battlemented, as at Stanton and Burford.

BRICK CHIMNEYS FROM NORFOLK

The progress and development of chimney-stacks provide an interesting study. They did not become common before the sixteenth century, and were called into being by the division of the great hall into an upper and a lower storey. The plan in smaller houses was square or oblong, and as the down draught was somewhat severe in these wide structures, the chimneys were built large and lofty, and in the Cotswold examples at Chipping Campden, Hidcote and Whittington were adorned at the summit with classic ornamentation.

As the Tudor style progressed, the stacks bear witness to

the great creative powers of the English builders, showing an unfailing exuberance of fancy in design and skill in workmanship. Whatever the material they used, whether stone, brick or terra-cotta, they tried to make this new feature of the house dignified, elegant and beautiful. It is impossible to say whence they procured the numerous designs of

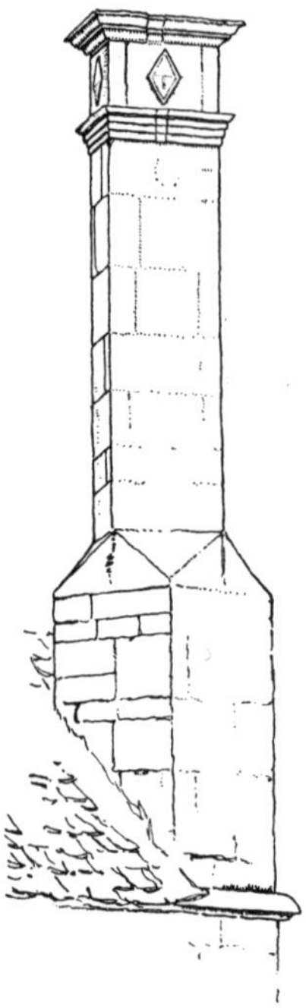

CHIPPING CAMPDEN

HIDCOTE

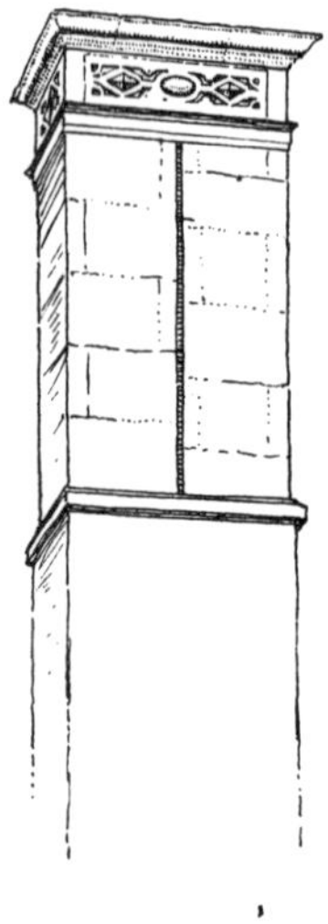

WHITTINGTON

patterned and twisted shafts. These were essentially English, as there is nothing like them in the contemporary buildings across the Channel.

The beautiful brick chimneys and chimney-stacks, among which are some most elaborate designs, add much to the general effect and grouping of the houses in East Anglia, some of the earlier examples at East Barsham, Elsing and Great Snoring being richly decorated with diaper or devices. The stack at East Barsham forms a group of ten chimneys made

BRICK CHIMNEYS FROM WARWICKSHIRE AND WORCESTERSHIRE

entirely of moulded brick ornamented with a great variety of patterns. The later examples are generally plain octagonal shafts as at Blakesley Hall, but with a variety of projecting caps and bases.

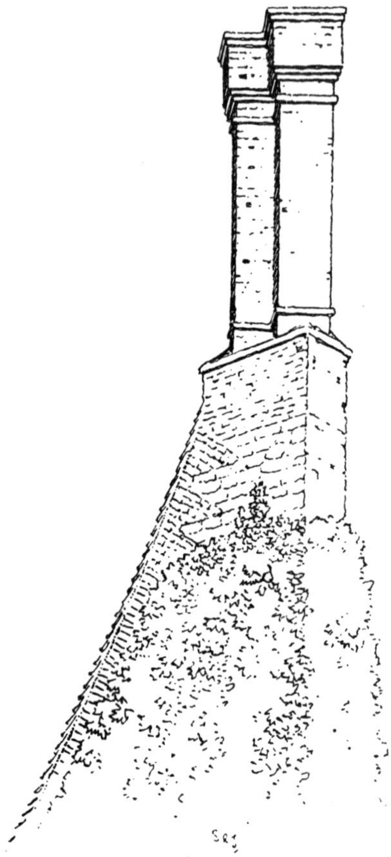

HEASLEY MANOR, ISLE OF WIGHT

In the Midlands we find the same effort in procuring variety of treatment, beauty and ornament. Huddington Court has a very elaborate chimney-stack with a pediment of Gothic character, from which rises a twisted shaft of moulded brick. Where the design is less elaborate, as at Great Alne, a good effect is produced by the insertion of tiles, the arrangement of corners of projecting bricks and other devices of the expert builder.

As the years rolled on new fashions set in, and practical considerations led the builders to see that these immense flues were not really required.

The illustration of the chimney on Escote Green, erected in 1669, shows that by about that time the chimney-stack had dwindled down to a compact block somewhat similar to our modern conceptions, though the arches and arcades of brickwork give to it a slightly ornamental character. We give some examples of southern stacks, showing the work of Isle of Wight artificers, which lack not comeliness and ingenuity.

Christopher Wren constructed many beautiful chimneys, but generally of small size and with no elaborate details. After his death the followers of the Italian school seemed to be ashamed of this important feature of the English house. In some of the great houses they tried to hide away the chimneys and keep them entirely in the background (see p. 38), and in the middle of the eighteenth century the importance of the chimney as a beautiful architectural accessory, upon which the Tudor builders bestowed so much loving care and skill, ceased to exist.

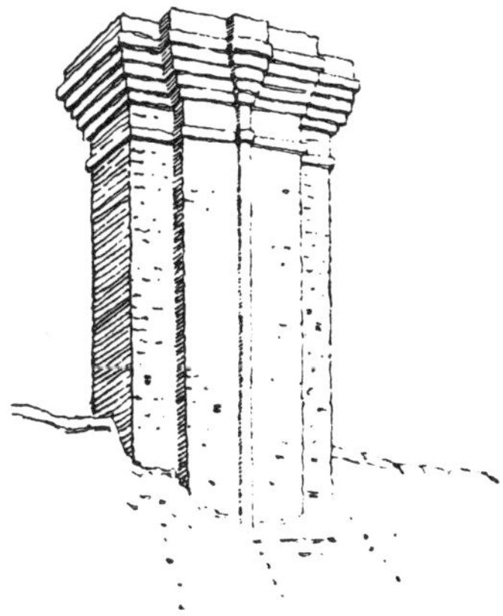

ST. BENEDICT'S PRIORY, KENT

2. PORCHES AND DOORS

The old English squire loved to dispense hospitality and to give warm welcome to his friends. The door was a symbol of hospitality. There he welcomed their arrival; there he speeded his departing guests. He loved to make the entrance to his house fair and pleasant to the eye. From the steps he greeted his tenantry when they came to congratulate him on some happy event in his domestic life, or to condole with him in his sorrows; and there in the proudest moment of his life he stood to present his young son on the youth's coming of age, happy that the old line had not died out and that his son would maintain the honour of the family and carry on its old traditions. The porch and doorway were associated with many happy comings and goings, and some sad ones too. It held a place of honour in the old manor-house.

In our chapter on the development of the English house

COOMBE SYDENHAM, SOMERSET

THE ENTRANCE TO WORMLEIGHTON MANOR-HOUSE
WARWICKSHIRE, DATED 1613

we noticed that the doorway always led to the screens. It was thought worthy of a covering to protect from the weather those who knocked for entrance. Over the door the squire placed his coat-of-arms with mantlings, crest and supporters. The porch increased in size and a chamber was built over it, and it became an important feature of the Tudor manor-house or mansion, completing the plan of the **E**-shaped house. Barningham Hall, in Norfolk, erected in 1612, has

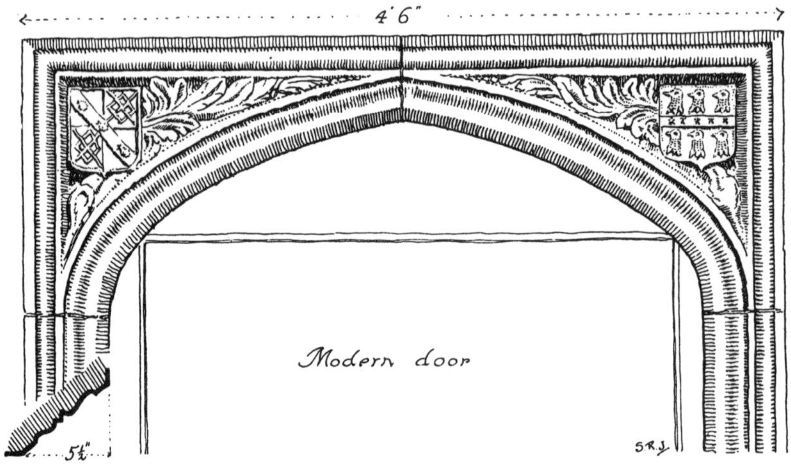

A STONE DOOR-HEAD AT WORMLEIGHTON MANOR

a grand four-storeyed porch in the centre of the west front. Burlingham St. Edmund has an elaborate porch, a very characteristic bit of Tudor work in three storeys, with octagonal angle turrets, which, together with the gable, are finished with rich finials. Kirstead (p. 95) has a three-storeyed porch with an arched and pedimented entrance doorway over which appears the date 1614. It has octagonal angle turrets with a three-light window between them, and a small single light in the gable.

In the West Country there are many inviting doorways bidding us a hospitable welcome. The manor-house of

Coombe Sydenham, in Somerset, has a noble porch of two storeys. It is Jacobean with classical pilasters supporting a decorated string-course. In the spandrels of the doorway are carved heads. Above the string and below the mullioned window is the coat-of-arms of the owners, and ball finials crown the angles and gable which is of low elevation. A very pretty piece of work is the admirable porch and entrance of Wolverton Manor in the Isle of Wight (p. 83), and joining on to the region of the Cotswolds is Wormleighton Manor-house, which we have already visited (p. 89). Here we notice its beautiful porch, dated 1613, and bearing the Spencer coat-of-arms. Adjoining it is the clock tower, and although you can see no face, it regularly strikes the hours and the quarters. A typical Tudor door head from the same house is also illustrated.

A PORCH, SULGRAVE, NORTHANTS

Near at hand is the little village of Sulgrave, Northamptonshire, once the home of the Washingtons, and here is a charming porch, dated 1636, with a sundial over the door. The four-centred arch of the doorway, the Tudor dripstone and the neat gable make an attractive entrance to the house,

The dark stone is interspersed with the lighter material. This is the ironstone of the district which runs with the Cotswold oolite, and is peculiar to Northamptonshire.

THE ENTRANCE DOOR, THE OLD HALL, BARNHAM BROOM NORFOLK

The two-storeyed entrance porch of some of the later manor-houses of the Tudor period often show evidence of classical inspiration, and the "orders" were employed as mere decorative adjuncts. "Such details disclosed a whimsical incongruity in the attempts to imitate features which were becoming 'fashionable,' although imperfectly understood. This breaking out into hybrid classicism, when the whole structure is otherwise homely Tudor, appears to be the result of the

AT WOOTON WAWEN, WARWICKSHIRE

second wave of architectural renaissance which came from Germany. The builders of the day, not sufficiently daring or skilful to fling aside their traditional methods, but desirous of showing that they were not trammelled by insular notions, availed themselves of the Flemish pattern books which could be readily purchased at Antwerp and cheaply copied at home.

Whereas in the larger mansions of the time of Elizabeth this led to a coarseness and ostentation which are frequently displeasing, in the smaller houses these very imperfections are not without their attraction and human appeal."[1]

THE MANOR-HOUSE AT ATWORTH, WILTSHIRE

We give an illustration of the entrance door of Barnham Broom Old Hall, a fine example of English woodwork, with its mouldings and panels showing a good specimen of the linen pattern, the origin of which we will discuss when we come to examine the inner panelling of our old manor-houses.

[1] *Domestic Architecture of England during the Tudor Period*, by T. Garner and Arthur Stratton.

In the later manor-houses and other domestic dwellings the porch ceased to have that prominence which the Tudor builders gave to it. Inigo Jones, Wren and his successors completely altered its appearance, took away its sides, placed a modest circular roof on supporting brackets and elaborately carved the tympanum with foliage and other devices. We have seen a good example of the shell porch in the Crown House, Newport, Essex (p. 107). We give another example from Wooton Wawen, Warwickshire, a Queen Anne type with modelled fruit over the door. The sketch of the gateway, with porch and door, at Atworth, in Wiltshire, shows a classic development which is observable in the neighbourhood of Bath.

The doorway, for reasons which I have mentioned, has always been the object of the greatest solicitude on the part of our builders, and upon it the best workmanship is most often found. If there be no ornament elsewhere, some effort seems always to have been made to make the doorway attractive and beautiful.

ROUND A DOOR FRAME

3. WINDOWS

Old houses have usually small windows. This is partly accounted for by the closeness of the timber framing, and also by the scarcity and cost of glass. Aubrey tells that "Glass windows, except in churches and gentlemen's houses, were rare before the time of Henry VIII. In my own remembrance, before the Civil Wars, copy holders and poor people had none in Herefordshire, Monmouthshire and Salop: it is so still." The old name "window" discloses this lack of glass; it is the eye, or opening, for the wind; and was originally constructed more for the admission of air than of light. Sometimes we see the remains of the wooden shutters or their iron hinges. Noblemen who had three or four houses used to carry their windows about with them with their other baggage. Sometimes horn was used in lieu of glass. There is an old account amongst the manuscripts preserved at Loseley Park, Surrey, of the time of Henry VIII, which has several items relating to horn for windows. Thus we read, "a thousand lantern horns for the windows of timber houses"; and again, "gilding the lead or lattice work of the horn windows."

In the days of Elizabeth windows became larger and were filled with glass. Bacon inveighed against the large windows of some houses, "so full of glass that one cannot tell where to become to be out of the sun or cold," and when Bess of Hardwick built her mansion the wits said of it:—

> Hardwick Hall,
> More glass than wall.

Many of the illustrations show charming windows that give light to the interiors of our manor-houses and form pleasing features of the exterior views. Bay, oriel, mullioned, latticed, or dormer, they are all beautiful, save the modern sash window which has been too often inserted in place of older and more excellent work. In the Cotswold region the windows are always stone mullioned, with lead-latticed panes and wrought-iron casements. A hood-moulding runs over each window, returning at each side after the Tudor fashion, and is sometimes extended so as to form a string-course. We have already noticed that the number of lights in the windows decreases in each succeeding storey. In many of the seventeenth-century houses the heads are arched, forming little spandrels on each side, causing them to resemble Perpendicular panels. These windows are set flush with the wall, so as to form on the inside those charming deep recesses which make pleasant seats like those we remember in many an Oxford College.

Bay windows are always charming whether in stone or timber houses. It was usual to emphasize the dais end of the hall by a bay on one or both sides of the house. Such windows are seen in the hall of Christ Church, Oxford, and of many other colleges, and at Ballingdon, Essex (p. 110).

Oriel windows frequently appear corbelled out from the main wall, as shown in the illustration. They are often supported on brackets built into the wall. We give an illustration of a bracket at Huddington.

WINDOW BRACKET

Sometimes the bay windows are brought out square from the front of the house, and are sometimes set in the centre of the gable, as in the case of Shipton Manor (p. 57) and Whittington (p. 5); but this arrangement is unsatisfactory, and appears awkward and unpleasing.

Dormers are a characteristic feature of the Cotswolds. The origin of dormers, whether in stone or timber houses, is evident. When the floor of the uppermost storey was inserted some three or four feet from the foot of the roof there was no room for the windows under the eaves; hence the side walls were carried up and a series of smaller gables constructed with windows in them. There are good examples of dormers at Brad Street, Kent (p. 83), and at Nunupton, Herefordshire (p. 102).

Later dormers were constructed entirely in the roof, as at Penn (p. 104) and Kirstead (p. 95).

In East Anglia we find the Gothic traditions closely followed in the windows. Some of the lights have the flat-arched Tudor head, and others have three-centred arches with labels over the windows.

In the sixteenth century we find square heads with labels over them, having square terminations or returns. In the seventeenth they have moulded pediments over them. Mullions and transoms were used throughout the Tudor and early Stuart times; the common arrangement consisted of two lights one above the other; some have three, but the smaller manor-houses have only mullioned windows of three, four or five lights.

A WINDOW FROM NORFOLK IN MOULDED BRICK

In half-timber houses the construction was simple. They were merely openings left between puncheons and transoms of the timber construction. The frames were beautifully moulded by the hand of the craftsman. In the larger houses the windows were transomed. Bay windows in the Surrey and Kent timber houses are not earlier than the seventeenth and eighteenth centuries, and lack the grace of the earlier joinery.

4. ROOFS AND GABLES

None of the manor-houses we have seen are roofed with the humble thatch. This picturesque roofing was reserved for smaller dwelling-places. The material used, of course, differs in various parts of the country. Tiles are perhaps the most common, which when mellowed by age, with moss and lichens growing upon them, form one of the chief charms of an English landscape. Much ingenuity has been exercised in the construction of these roofs, and most picturesque are they in their grouping and arrangement. You can recognize the earlier roofs by their steepness. The later sixteenth-century roof was much flatter. Another sign of early work is the long uninterrupted sweep of the roof without dormer windows or gables and terminated by hips. The hips are extended over the lean-to buildings. As we have already pointed out, the walls of timber framed houses were frequently hung with tiles, but these are lighter and smaller than those used for roofing; and the old tiles are thicker and more unevenly burnt than modern ones. The wall tiles were usually plain or of the "fish scale" pattern, which consists of the lower halves of circles connected by a short horizontal piece, and overlapping the row beneath. Sometimes they were arranged in diversified patterns, as in the illustration. Modern machine-made tiles can never equal the old handmade products. There is a picturesque unevenness about the laying of these old tiles. Their varying colour adds to the beauty of the roofs and produces a peculiar and subtle charm. There

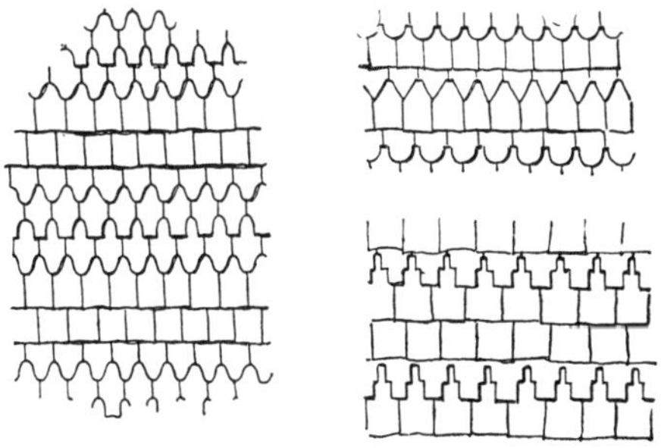

HANGING TILE PATTERNS FROM SURREY AND SUSSEX

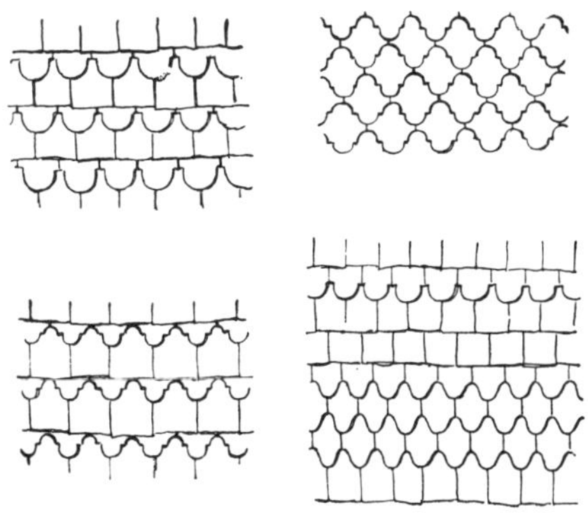

HANGING TILE PATTERNS

is a great variety in old ridge-tiling, and the saddle-back hip tiles at the junction of two planes of the roof are a notable feature.

Horsham slabs were extensively used in Sussex and in the neighbouring counties. This stone easily flakes into plates like thick slates and forms large grey flat slabs on which "the weather works like a great artist in harmonies of moss, lichen and stain. No roofing so combines dignity and homeliness, and no roofing except thatch so surely passes into the landscape." It is to be regretted that this stone is no longer used for roofing. The slabs are somewhat thick and heavy, and modern rafters are not adapted to bear their weight. If you want to have a roof of Horsham stone you can only accomplish your purpose by pulling down an old house and carrying off the slates. Perhaps the small Cotswold stone slabs are even more beautiful, and the old halls of Lancashire and Yorkshire have heavy stone roofs which somewhat resemble those fashioned with Horsham slabs. We have already noticed the ingenuity of the builders who adapted the slope of the roof to the materials they used. They observed that when the sides of the roof were deeply sloping the heavy stone slates strained and dragged at the pegs and laths, and fell and injured the roof. Hence they determined to make the slope less steep, and when the rain refused to run off well and penetrated the house they adopted the plan of cementing their roofs and stopped them with mortar.

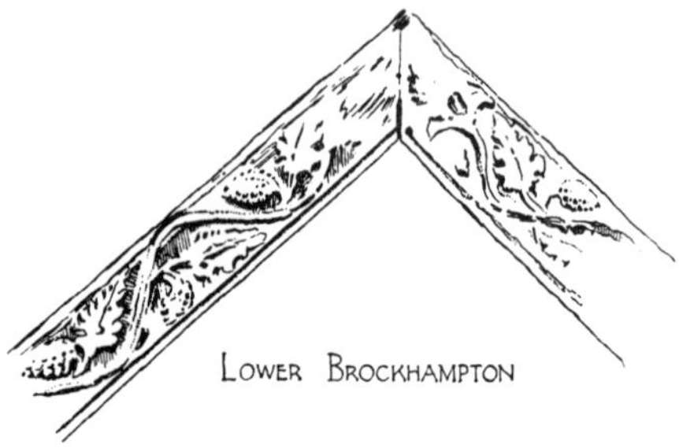

LOWER BROCKHAMPTON

The construction of the roofs of our manor-houses is an interesting study, and testifies to the conservatism of the

English workman. The carpenters of the sixteenth and seventeenth centuries followed closely in the footsteps of the

GABLE, HANDFORTH HALL, CHESHIRE

mediæval craftsman. They preserved the tradition handed down to them by their forefathers, and framed hammer-beam roofs, king-posts, collar-beams with purlins and all the intricacies of the ingeniously constructed house-covering after the fashion of their ancestors.

We have frequently alluded to the gables that adorn our houses and are such attractive features. In timber-framed houses the gables are flush with

MERSTONE, ISLE OF WIGHT

the roof, and have projecting barge-boards, of which we give some examples. The wide projection was for the purpose of protecting the walls from rain. Much ingenuity was expended in their construction and decoration. We have already noticed that in mediæval and early Renaissance times they were cut into curves and cusps at the edges. In the sixteenth century they were pierced with tracery in the form of trefoils or quatrefoils, and in the seventeenth the perforated designs are more fantastic, and correspond to the details of Jacobean carving. The Bridgnorth example on p. 69 is dated 1580. The barge-boards are simple in design, but much labour has been bestowed upon the panelled structure with the curved braces. The Lower Brockhampton gable is later.

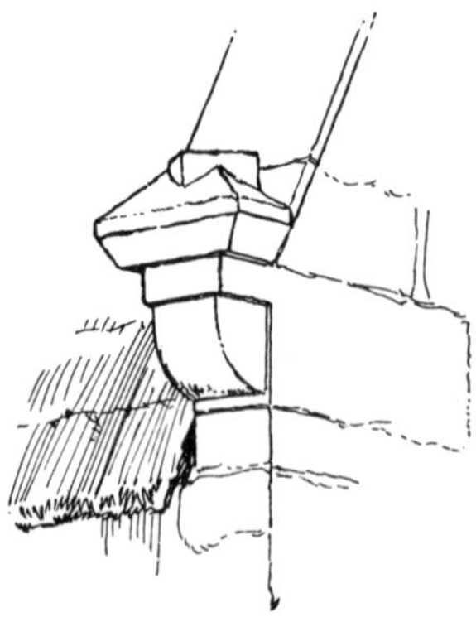

AT MORETON PINKNEY

A very fine gable is shown in the illustration of Handforth Hall, a house which we have already visited, one of Cheshire's fine black and white buildings. As the inscription states, the main part of the house was built in 1562, but it is not all timber and plaster now, some parts having been encased in brick and painted to represent the old style. This gable, however, is original, and is a fine piece of construction.

WOLVERTON, ISLE OF WIGHT

In stone and brick houses the gable wall rises above the roof, and is coped with stone to prevent the wet penetrating into it. The coping rests at the bottom upon a kneeler, and is crowned at the apex by a finial. Examples of kneelers are

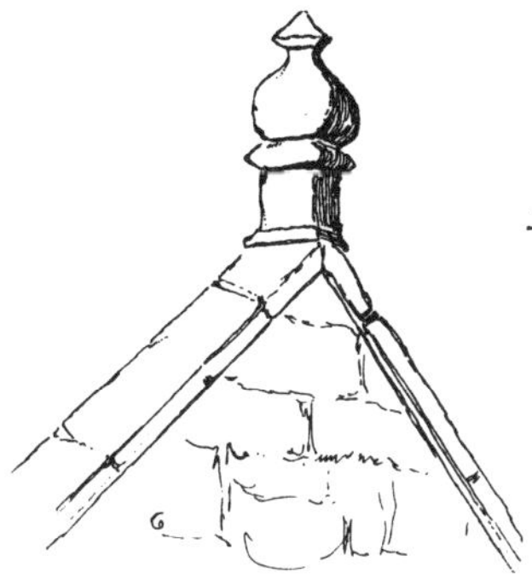

KINGSTON, ISLE OF WIGHT

OWLPEN, GLOUCESTERSHIRE

shown in the illustrations taken from Moreton Pinkney and Merstone and Wolverton, both in the Isle of Wight. In Jacobean times the kneelers as well as the apex of the

AT MERSTONE
ISLE OF WIGHT

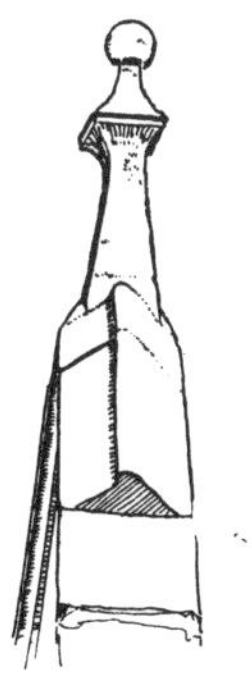

MOOR HALL
GLOUCESTERSHIRE

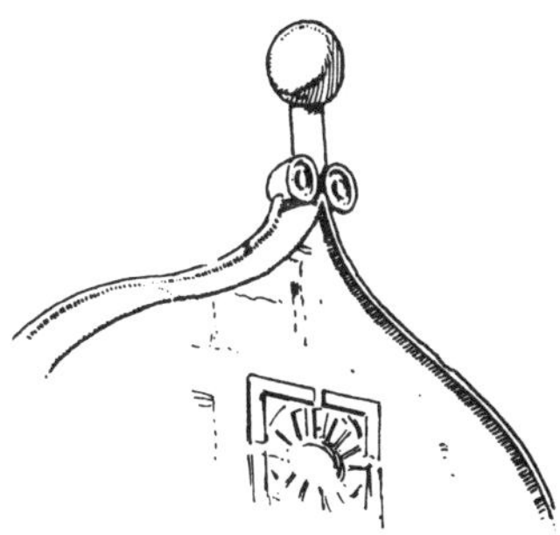

OWLPEN
GLOUCESTERSHIRE

gable were adorned with finials. A considerable amount of variety was introduced into the design of finials and kneelers, and examples of several of them are given from some of the houses which we have already seen—Whittington, Moor Hall, Kingston and Merstone, Owlpen and Hidcote.

WHITTINGTON GLOUCESTER-SHIRE

In the eastern counties we find some beautiful moulded work in brick. Below we see a bold attempt at decoration, the crow-steps and the turrets at the end of the gable. These turrets seem to have been of no practical utility, and are placed there purely for ornamental purposes. The little cornice is beautifully moulded. We have given several examples of crow-steps, another result of foreign influence, which impart a not unpleasing effect to many picturesque gables.

The example from Owlpen shows the curved gable which was originally introduced into England by the Flemish immigrants. We have already seen many houses with this feature, but of a more elaborate character, with segments of circles alternated with straight pieces.

BRICK DETAILS FROM NORFOLK

The English mason did not admire these fantastic gables which the Dutchman loved, and tried to simplify them. Only in large mansions, like Wollaton, do we find this foreign influence strongly developed, where the masons seem to have determined to leave no single bit of plain surface on the walls. Projecting bands, pedestals, pilasters, panels, niches, pediments, fantastic gables, obelisks and statues contribute to this mass of over-decoration which was distasteful to English simplicity, and which finds no place in the houses that we love to admire.

THE BOUDOIR, RAYNHAM HALL, NORFOLK

VI

INTERIOR DETAILS

THE hospitable door of the manor-house invites an entrance, and we will at once proceed to inspect its interior treasures of art and architectural beauty. We enter through the porch and door that leads to the "screens," and then through a door in the same which leads to the hall. According to the usual arrangement, the buttery, kitchen and servants' quarters are on the right as we enter if the hall is on the left hand. The illustration of Ditcheat Priory (p. 29) shows this plan. In this instance there are two buttery hatches. The screen on the left is evidently Jacobean work and bears the date 1613, but the house is much older, having been built by John Grimthorpe in 1473. It was one of the principal manors of Glastonbury Abbey, and was frequently occupied by the abbot. It is now the seat of General Leir-Carleton, who has done much to restore its original features. The floor of this passage was paved with tiles, but he has recently refloored it with stone after the ancient manner. The three coats-of-arms on the end wall over the table are modern.

We have seen the exterior of the Gloucestershire manor-house of Whittington Court, with its graceful gables, built by Richard Cotton in the first half of the sixteenth century. Here is a view of the entrance hall with its old nail-studded door divided into panels, its panelling and old-time furniture. The house has been carefully restored, and the archway

THE ENTRANCE HALL, WHITTINGTON COURT, GLOUCESTERSHIRE

STANTON OLD HALL, DERBYSHIRE

in front of the drawing is modern. The sun shining through the open door can scarcely look upon a fairer home. Some of the details of this house we shall notice later.

WORMLEIGHTON MANOR, WARWICKSHIRE

The interior of Stanton Old Hall shows the severe yet dignified plainness of a north-country dwelling, and, unlike the rich decoration inside Cartledge Hall (p. 166), corresponds exactly with the quiet exterior illustrated on p. 49. The room at Raynham Hall, Norfolk, is given to show a charming typical interior of the later Renaissance, which it is interesting to compare with the Jacobean rooms illustrated. The house, an undoubted example of the work of Inigo Jones, was built as early as 1636, though the type of work it heralded did not become general till after the Restoration.

Wormleighton Manor, in Warwickshire, the home of the Spencers, has already been visited (pp. 89 and 123). This interior doorway is a characteristic feature with the arms of the family above. These are beautifully wrought in relief, but the shields have unfortunately been "picked out" by the village painter. Not much respect has been shown to the appearance of the doorway, or to the right-hand shield, as the wall on the right has been built into the doorway in order to make a bathroom, which, however necessary, ought

THE KITCHEN, KINGSTON MANOR, ISLE OF WIGHT

not to have obscured the appearance of this noble door or obliterate half of the coat-of-arms.

The plain interior of Kingston Manor, with its uneven stone-flagged floor and long table, is now used as a kitchen, though it is surmised that at one time it formed part of the original hall, long since divided.

I. MANTELPIECES AND FIREPLACES

The story of the gradual introduction of fireplaces has already been partially told. We have seen the smoke emerging from the louvre, the first building of a fireplace in the solar, the great open yawning chimney in the hall, the huge fireplace and dog-grate. The Tudor builders began to bestow much elaboration upon their chimney-pieces, which were fashioned of wood or stone, or—in the great houses—of marble. There is an immense variety in their construction and ornamentation. An architectural expert thus well describes them: "The idea was to flank the fireplace

AT WHITTINGTON COURT

opening with columns carrying an entablature consisting of architrave, frieze and cornice, the projection of the latter forming a convenient shelf. On the top of this composition was another of the same kind, but with smaller columns and more delicate proportion. The space enclosed between the columns, which in the lower half was the fireplace, was occupied in the upper half by some kind of carved subject. This was very often the arms of the family, or his own special achievement."[1] Until the time of Elizabeth these mantel-

[1] *Early Renaissance Architecture in England*, by J. Alfred Gotch.

pieces were fairly simple in design and were characterized by refinement and a suppression of elaborate ornament, but the German masons, who found much work in England, introduced coarse and ridiculous details, and "the incessant repetition of the same trick of design suggests the hand of the

A STONE MANTELPIECE, WHITTINGTON COURT

tradesman rather than the artist, the German pattern book rather than the fresh spontaneous fancy of the English designer of the sixteenth century."[1] There are, however, some wonderful mantelpieces at South Wraxall, Loseley, Cobham, Hatfield, and the finest in England are at Knole.

The illustrations of the mantelpieces at Whittington Court made of stone show the character of the earlier work. In

[1] *Renaissance Architecture in England*, by R. Blomfield.

SHELDON HALL, WARWICKSHIRE

A PLASTER CHIMNEYPIECE, SOMERSET

Jacobean times the decoration became more elaborate, as the plaster fireplace and overmantel from a house in Somerset, erected in 1629, plainly show. A very characteristic Jacobean oak carved mantel exists at Sheldon Hall, Warwickshire, with a stone opening.

Our ancestors were fond of figure subjects for their mantelpieces. One of the illustrations shows two ponderous figures of men clad in armour. Other figures are frequently

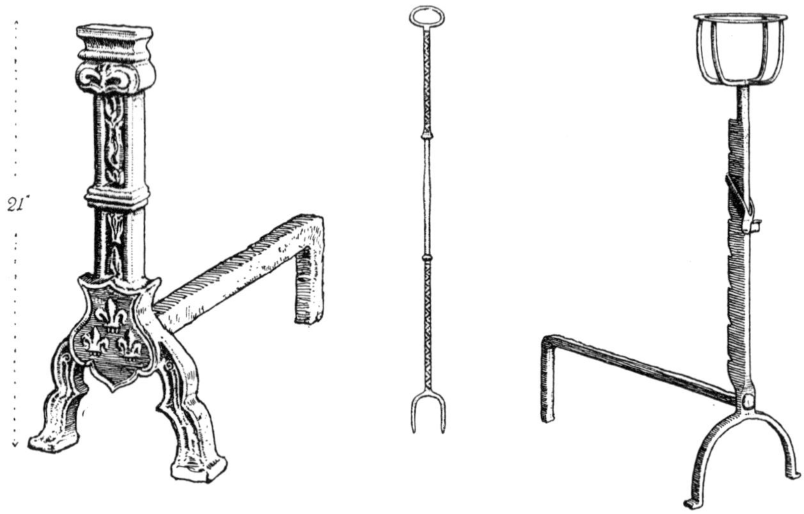

DOGS AND TOASTING FORK AT WARNHAM COURT, SUSSEX
From the collection of Mr. P. J. Lucas

found, especially in large and important houses. At South Wraxall manor-house there is an elaborate stone chimneypiece. Pairs of caryatides adorned with flowers hold up the lower entablature, and above are statues representing Arithmetica, Geometria, Prudentia and Justicia. Apollo and the Nine Muses appear at Hardwick Hall with E.R., and the Queen's supporters, the lion and dragon. Subjects taken from Holy Scripture are not unusual, such as Christ blessing little Children, the Descent from the Cross, the Lamentation over Jerusalem, the Agony in the Garden, and the Troubles of Job. Latin mottoes, of which the Elizabethans seem to have been very fond, are frequently inscribed along the lower entablature.

The Somerset plaster example shown in the illustration is not the only specimen of the art of the parge-worker employed in the making of mantelpieces. An interesting one is found at Calgarth Old Hall, Windermere. Two shields, with armorial bearings and crests above, occupy the main filling of the panels, and at the top is the motto FIDE NON FRAUD. The manor-house of West Down, North Devon, has some wonderful plaster mantels, representing some strange event which it seems difficult to identify. There is a winged figure in a chariot drawn by two very spirited horses, a church on a hill in the distance, several figures walking in procession, and two colossal figures on each side of the large panel, one of which holds an anchor. Here is a strange riddle for the solution of the curious reader. The true interpretation may be as follows :—The general subject symbolizes Human Life. The car drawn by antelopes is the Triumph of Time. The other figures, beginning with the go-cart, are the Ages of Human Life, of which there are six. The figures carrying baskets on their heads, flowers in one and fruit in the other, refer to the beginning and end of life, possibly symbolizing Spring and Autumn. The anchor is the symbol of hope in

A FIREBACK AT LOUGHTON HALL, ESSEX

the future for the nascent life. The figure holding a disk, or mirror, is a symbol of the vanity of life. The church in a walled enclosure represents Religion, and probably its upper portion means the New Jerusalem. Here is the crown of life and its future. The artist has combined several notions and fancies, but his subject is made up of old ideas, and this is often found in the work of the sixteenth century. The famous Plas Mawr, Conway, has

AN EARLY FIREBACK

some remarkable plaster-work. It was the home of the Wynne family, who entertained Queen Elizabeth and commemorated the royal visit by much elaborate decoration. One mantel is divided by beads into nine panels, flanked by enriched turret-like three-quarter pillars, the royal arms, bearers and crown on the central panel, and E.R. on shields on the left and right. The other panels are filled with rosettes and bosses. A chained portcullis appears in the top left-hand panel. In the banqueting-hall there is a mantel made up of all the ornaments used in the ceilings of all the rooms in the house. Another mantel has E.R. in large letters, one on each side of a rosette girt by the garter with the motto HONI SOIT QUI MAL Y PENSE. Two weird caryatides stand on each side of the mantel. Yet another mantel has a huge shield of arms, quartered three stags' heads, three spread eagles, three *fleurs-de-lis*, three masks with chevron, and the initials R.G. and date 1567. Later on the art of the plasterer exercised itself more on the ceilings of the rooms than on the mantelpieces.

An important adjunct to the fireplace were the firedogs and firebacks. In some Norman fireplaces these were absent; there is no recess for their accommodation. The back of the fireplace sloped backwards from the base as at Conisborough Castle, and the logs must have been placed on end against the slope. The oldest firedogs now in existence, with rare exceptions, are not earlier than the fifteenth century, and these have I.H.S. inscribed upon their upright standards, and may have been used in some monastery. In Tudor and Elizabethan houses there were always dogs and backs of an immense variety of design. We give one example from Loughton Hall, Essex, and some from the collection of Mr. C. J. Lucas, of Warnham Court, Sussex. One of them is a cup-dog for placing a cup of mulled ale in the framework at the top, which could be raised or lowered. The backs are of cast iron, and usually the arms of the family are cast on them. In the region of Sussex, once the "Black Country" of England, where iron ore was plentiful, many curious backs are discovered in farm or manor-house.

2. STAIRCASES

In mediæval houses the staircase was similar to that in an old church tower and was placed at the dais end of the hall in a turret. You ascended the stone steps which wound round the centre shaft or newel. A spiral staircase of this kind King Henry III erected for his palace at Clarendon.

Little Wenham Hall, erected in the time of the first Edward, had in one corner of the tower a turret with a newel staircase. At Penshurst you can still see the open archway at the dais end of the hall leading to the upper fourteenth-

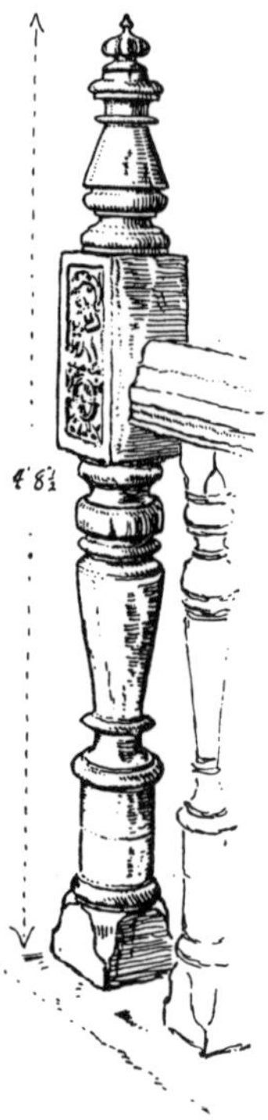

SHELDON HALL

STAIRCASE NEWELS, HARVINGTON HALL WORCESTERSHIRE

century rooms. These were the usual staircases of mediæval times. Those of the sixteenth century resembled them and were of the "corkscrew" type, built of stone or brick and destitute of ornament. The story of the subsequent progress of the staircase is remarkable. The builders of our houses

HALL I' TH' WOOD, TONGE, LANCASHIRE

suddenly broke away from all preceding traditions. The old stone newel turret staircases were abandoned. Perhaps our old squires and gentry grew tired of mounting these interminable steps. Perhaps some of the foreign masons told them of some wonderful staircases which they had in their own country in the châteaux in the valley of the Loire. Perhaps the famous John Thorpe devised their plan out of his ingenious brain. He has left us some good designs and drawings of staircases now preserved in the Soane Museum, and there are many actual staircases constructed in accordance with these plans. Ere long in many a manor-house arose a broad staircase of oak with heavily carved newels, pierced balustrading and rich carving. It was generally placed in connection with the hall and lends to the interior an air of spaciousness and dignity. Its importance arises from the fact that the chief living-rooms were often placed on the upper floor, and therefore demanded a dignified means of approach.

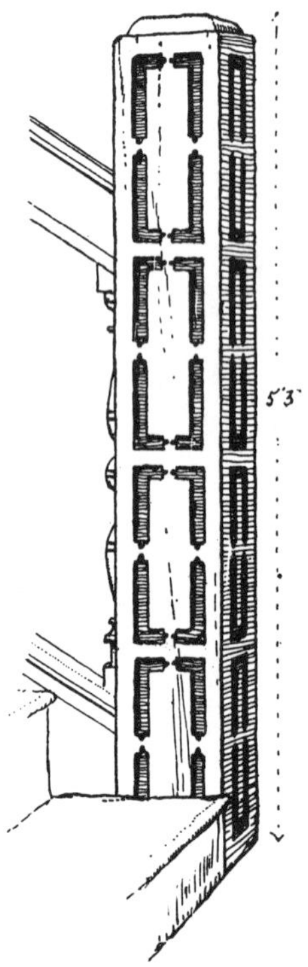

A NEWEL AT WHITTINGTON COURT

The idea of this staircase is really that of a glorified ladder. Instead of the sides of the ladder we have "strings," or narrow pieces of wood, and instead of rungs treads and risers forming steps. One string was fastened to the wall, and the foot of the other secured into a stout upright post, or newel, as also was the top; into the same newel that received the top of the first string the foot of the second was secured at right angles, this process being repeated as the staircase ascended. At about two feet above the top of the string, and parallel to it, was

SHELDON HALL, WARWICKSHIRE

the handrail, and between the handrail and the string were balusters.[1] Thus were the early staircases constructed. The newels were massive, as you will see from the illustrations of those at Whittington Court, Harvington Hall and Sheldon Hall. Our ancestors were considerate for old people, and did not make long flights of steps. There were usually only six steps and then a landing. The staircases were arranged round a central well-hole, but in some cases this central well-hole was occupied by a solid block of masonry. The newels were decorated with carving, or with a pattern inscribed upon them, as in the Whittington example. The tops were usually raised high, as at Harvington, and carved figures were frequently placed upon them, as at Aldermaston Court.[2] Animals that appear in the armorial bearings of the family, warriors, boys playing instruments, Hercules and the Furies, and knights in armour, as at Hartwell, were some of the favourite subjects. The strings and handrails were carved with a pattern or moulded. The balusters were usually turned to resemble a pillar, or they were pierced with a design, or converted into a series of arches. The newels of the second and upward flights had pendants, as in the fine staircase at Hall i' th' Wood. Everything that art could devise was done to enrich the effect, and the ingenuity of the Jacobean carvers introduced further embellishments, rich panelling and other devices to enhance its stateliness. A good example of the Jacobean staircase is that at Sheldon Hall, of which we give an illustration. As it frequently led to the Great Chamber, which, besides being the principal chamber of the Elizabethan and Jacobean house and the chief resort of the family, was the place where the squire received his guests, it was made as attractive and perfect as possible.

[1] *Early Renaissance Architecture in England*, by J. A. Gotch.

[2] The old manor-house was burned down, but happily these carved figures were rescued and placed in the new mansion.

THE STAIRCASE, MELBOURNE HALL, DERBYSHIRE

The steps were made very wide, often six or seven feet, very different from the restricted stairs in modern houses, wherein often the element of cost is severely considered. They were shallow and easy of ascent, again differing from many modern stairs, to ascend which is good exercise, but brings little comfort to the aged and infirm; and their massive appearance and elaborate decoration gave dignity to the house.

When the Italian ideas influenced our English builders the design and conception of the staircase were changed. Instead of the stately designs of the Tudors the later imitators of the Palladian school introduced long continuous flights of winding stairs, frequently built into the wall, without any visible means of support on the other side. These were scarcely an improvement, and we prefer the older plan and arrangement. The eighteenth-century staircase at Melbourne Hall appears in our illustrations in order to show one of the finest achievements of the art of the period. It is not continuous; the balusters are varied, a plain one alternating with a spiral, and the whole effect is dignified and restful.

3. PANELLING

Our forefathers knew well how to make their houses comfortable, and no method was more effectual than by covering the walls with wood. Plaster walls covered with wall-paper always make the room draughty, chilling the air that has been warmed by the fire and thus creating a draught. Panelled rooms are always warm and snug and comfortable. Moreover, they are pleasant to the eye, especially when designed with all the skill and art of the Tudor carpenter.

The story of the development of panelling is interesting, but it would require more space than we can give to recount it fully. The earliest form of panel was much longer than that afterwards in use. In the fifteenth century much timber was required, the uprights of the frames being 4 inches in width and 3 inches in thickness. The uprights were 18 inches apart, cross-pieces being added at intervals of about 4 or 5 feet. The spaces were filled with boards, and the frames moulded on the upper and two sides, not at the bottom of the panel. The top of the panel was ornamented by cuspings. Possibly on account of the scarcity of timber

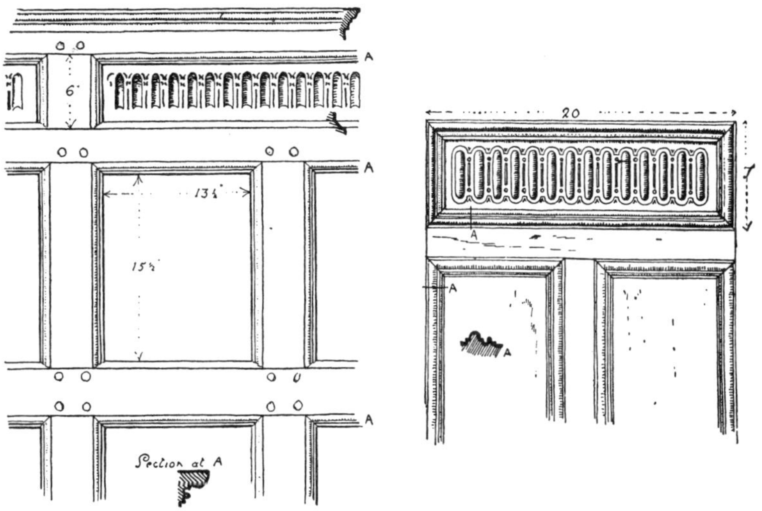

CARTLEDGE HALL HALL I TH WOOD

WOOD PANELLING

the size of the frames and panels was gradually decreased. The height of the panel in the illustration at Owlpen is about 17 inches by $12\frac{1}{2}$ inches, that at Cartledge $15\frac{1}{2}$ inches by $13\frac{1}{2}$ inches, and the thickness of the framing about one inch. The latter example shows that the panels assumed a square shape. The illustrations show also the characteristic mouldings of the period. Carving was used to decorate the panels. At Cartledge there is an interesting carved panel over the fireplace representing the sea, earth and sky, with the temptation of Adam and Eve. A very characteristic form of adornment was the linen-fold pattern, of which an illustration is gi,en on page 126. The history of this design has been ably traced by Mr. Aymer Vallance.[1] He has not discovered any examples earlier than the middle of the fifteenth century and believes that it was first devised by French or Flemish artists. It was not originally intended to imitate folded linen, but was evolved naturally out of the exigencies of joinery construction. It began in its simplest form with a vertical line branching out at either end into two oblique lines like a capital letter **Y**, upright at the top and inverted at the bottom. A slight curving in the arms of the **Y**

WOOD PANELLING

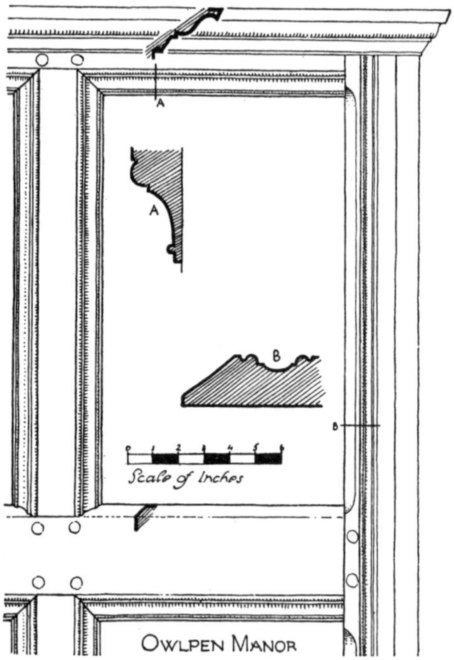

WOOD PANELLING

[1] *The Magazine of Fine Arts*, January, 1906.

produces the ogival outline of the extremities of the matured linen pattern. By degrees additional lines and folds were introduced, the ends decorated with ornament, until at last the pattern became exaggerated and less satisfactory. In its prime it was a very beautiful and effective design for adorning the surface of panels.

Heads were often carved in circular medallions on panels, the background being filled in with foliage. Later on, in Elizabethan times, it was fashionable to limit the carving and decoration to the top of the panelled surface and to leave the lower part entirely plain. The illustrations of the panels at Cartledge and of that at the Lancashire house of Hall i' th' Wood show this arrangement. In all this work the decoration was cut into the surface of panels. The Jacobean carpenter was very proud of his carving, and introduced into his panels round-headed arches with pilasters, imposts and bases decorated with the profusion of ornamental carving which delighted his soul. The illustration of the panelling at Sheldon Hall exhibits good examples of his skill.

CUPBOARD DOOR
KINGSTON MANOR, ISLE OF WIGHT

Instead of the natural beauty of oak timber, later on, fashion decreed that this dark panelling should be painted. White colour or light blue was favoured, and this barbarous custom existed for many years, and disfigured the original work left to us by our ancestors. We prefer now to remove these coatings of paint which a debased taste ordered to be smeared over the oaken panels, and to exhibit them in their natural beauty and condition.

The skill of the carpenter is shown also in the grand old cupboard doors, such as that at Kingston Manor in the Isle of Wight, in screens which were often elaborately decorated, in porches attached to rooms as at Broughton, Oxfordshire, chests and furniture as well as in mantelpieces, doorways and other interior details to which we have already referred.

CARTLEDGE HALL, DERBYSHIRE

A very unusual feature is shown in the illustration of an object in Cartledge Hall, Derbyshire. It is a clock-case constructed in the panelling and evidently of the same date. The side and front shown in the sketch, as well as the pierced top, are made to open all the way up. The pierced top allows the face of the clock to be seen.

Another way of covering the walls of rooms was the use of tapestry, and many old houses have most curious and valuable pieces stowed away in cupboards or still hanging on the walls. Few can tell their history, where they came from, or who designed and fashioned them, and many owners are in complete ignorance of the value of their possessions.

Not long ago in a country house on the top of a cupboard in the attics lay in dusty oblivion some pieces of tapestry that were worth £17,000.

4. CEILINGS

The art of the plasterer found a grand field for its exercise in the ceilings of the manor-houses and mansions, and so great were his skill and his energy, so eagerly was he sought after, that there are few houses of any note which have not some specimens of his handicraft. When Henry VIII invited to this country Italian plasterers who had been adorning their native palaces, they were attracted (as we have noticed) by the series of plastered panels of half-timber houses which cried aloud for decoration, and covered them with heraldic devices, figures, heads, foliage and other designs. The Italians taught the English folk the secret of their skill; but the English plasterer did not slavishly copy the designs of the Italian artist. After his fashion he developed the art on his own lines and according to his native sentiment, evolving his own plans and schemes and methods. He was a very important person, and had in London a Livery Company of his own, with a royal charter granted by Henry VII and confirmed by subsequent sovereigns. Good artists in plaster were in great request. Charles Williams, the most famous of our native craftsmen, who had studied the work of the foreigner in Italy, did some of the wondrous work for Henry's Palace of Nonsuch. Sir John Thynne secured his services for his noble house of Longleat, Wiltshire. The fame of his brilliant workmanship travelled far, and soon Sir William Cavendish and his lady, the renowned "Bess of Hardwick," were begging Sir John to send to them this cunning craftsman, who, they heard, had made "dyvers pendants and other pretty things, and had flowered the Hall at Longleat." In the early period of this art the English plasterer adopted as his first idea of a good ceiling a system

CARTLEDGE HALL CEILING

of interlacing squares with radial ribs. Then, with growing boldness, he made the ribs arched, and from their junction hung a pendant. At first painting was extensively used, but in the Elizabethan time it was entirely abandoned. Then curvilinear, interlacing and knotted forms appear, the ribs being embossed with running ornament, modelled or impressed. A fine adaptation of scroll-work is also a characteristic of the style.

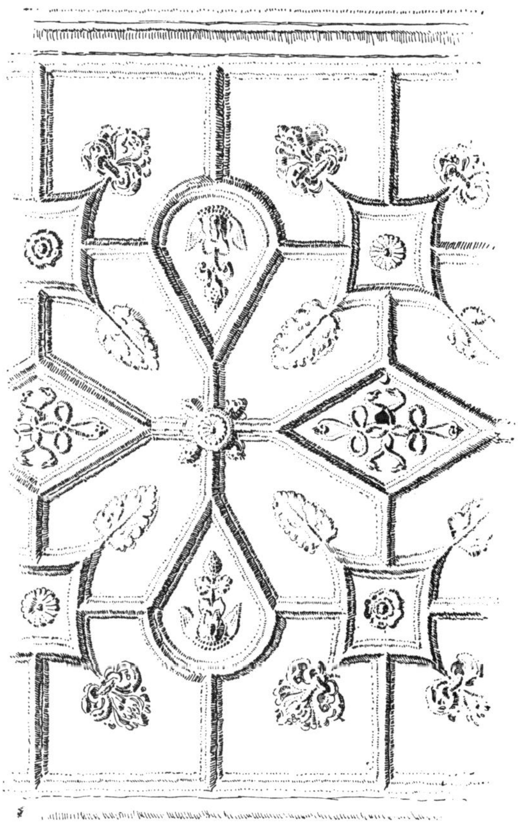

DETAIL OF THE CEILING
CARTLEDGE HALL

The plaster ceiling at Cartledge Hall, Derbyshire, belongs to this period, when so many of our noble English mansions were being erected, an age that gave birth to Hatfield, Longleat, Audley End, Chatsworth, Hardwick and many other of the grandest English seats. Cartledge Hall stands on a high and desolate moorland, and externally is homely and unpretentious, but picturesque. The interior is remarkable for its oak panelling and rich plaster-work. The room illustrated is divided lengthwise by a long beam, which is plastered over, mouldings being formed on the sides and a running pattern on the under side. The ornamental ceiling on the half next the fireplace has unfortunately fallen in, and this defacement greatly detracts from the rich appearance the room must originally have possessed. The pattern of ribs is typical of Early Renaissance work, and the squares are ornamented at each corner with leaves or *fleurs-de-lis*, while the panels are filled with rosettes or twisted knots and snakes. The design, though without anything specially dis-

WARREN HOUSE, STANTON, GLOUCESTERSHIRE

tinctive about it, is quietly effective, but a far richer ceiling exists in another room. This is coved to form a variety of curved surfaces, and one side is a spreading vine tree, filling in the panels which support the ceiling ribs, which is balanced on the other by the model of an oak tree, springing from the angle of the room, with a squirrel sitting on one of the branches. The bleak exterior of the house (p. 52) does not prepare us for the beauty of the interior decoration, of which the fine oak panelling is a charming feature.

It was customary to fasten the ceilings to thick laths made

of oak. This thickness of the laths is a sign of early work. The plasterers of later times used thinner laths, as they found that the plaster pressed between the laths gained a firmer hold. The earlier artificers used reeds and fibre or

THE OLD HOUSE, SANDWICH, KENT

rye straw as a foundation of their work ; but the abundance of fine cow-hair used in the construction of later works of art did away with the necessity of such aids. The tenacity of this cow-hair is certainly remarkable. In the projected portions of the ceilings there is a considerable quantity, the hair being more generously used there than in the other parts. Many ceilings have stood for three centuries without developing a crack, much more without falling. Modern ceilings, as ordinarily contracted for, endure about four years, then develop cracks, and down they fall. The cause of this is that modern builders do not introduce the same amount of hair into the plaster, and are content to use for an entire ceiling that which would scarcely have sufficed for a single square foot of an ancient one.

The ceiling at Warren House, Stanton, is also Elizabethan, constructed about the year 1590, and the very beautiful example from the Old House, Sandwich, shows a development of design and is Jacobean of the date about 1610. The method of construction is interesting. The heavier ceilings were first floated up in plain plaster, and then the finishing coat with all the projections downward put on afterwards. The tenacity of the hair allowed of this being done with safety, but the first coat was left very rough in order to support the second, and the power of the adherence of the latter must have been very great. The moulded portions were what architects call "run," that is, worked by a trammel, and then the enrichments stamped in the soft plaster.

With Inigo Jones came a new style of plaster ceiling which was formed on Italian models. He used heavy moulded ribs of far greater size than in the preceding period. The designs were stiffer and more cumbrous, such as the ceiling of the salon in Raynham Hall, Norfolk. Paintings began to be used in the centre of the ceiling surrounded by plaster-work, as in the illustration of the fine ceiling at Potheridge House, Torrington, Devonshire. Some details of the modillioned cornice are not unlike that in the White Room at Westwood Park, near Droitwich, Worcestershire, erected before the time of Grinling Gibbons, and it can be classed with other good work of the kind in this country. The modelling is free and good and is certainly the work of a skilful hand. During Wren's time English

POTHERIDGE HOUSE, TORRINGTON, NORTH DEVON

plaster-work flourished, and many extraordinarily good ceilings were wrought. After his death it deteriorated rapidly. Cornices, friezes and architraves were enriched with meaningless ornaments. Italian workmen came to England when William III reigned, and the fashions of Versailles ruled the style, but the work of the English plasterer, who imitated the foreigner, was less delicate and more clumsy. During the eighteenth century the brothers Adam introduced a new style which was graceful and refined, but lacked originality. They were very proud of their work, and one of them not very modestly declared: "We have introduced a great diversity of ceilings, friezes, and decorated pilasters, and have added grace and beauty to the whole, by a mixture of grotesque stucco and painted ornaments, together with the flowing *rainceau* with its fanciful figures and winding foliage. If we have any claim to approbation, we found it on this alone: that we flatter ourselves we have been able to seize with some degree of success the beautiful spirit of antiquity, and to inform it with novelty and variety, through all our numerous works." True artists are seldom satisfied with their work. Perhaps Master Adam was an exception. In the nineteenth century plaster-work suffered with other arts, and now, at last, shows signs of a true revival.

5. WINDOWS

We have already admired the windows of the house, their mullions and transoms, and other architectural features. Bay, oriel, dormer, all give diversity to the plan and structure of the manor-house. We may add a few words about the glazing. Much of the beautiful glass that once adorned their windows has perished, but some has been wonderfully preserved. When visiting Great Chalfield Manor, a house that was almost a ruin until it was rescued from its deplorable condition by the present owner, Mr. R. Fuller, we discovered high up in an upstairs room a fragment of ancient glass with the inscription :—

> Love God, and drede shame;
> Desire, worship and kepe Thy Name.

Ockwells Manor, near Bray, Berkshire, has a unique series of beautiful windows contemporary with the house, which was built by Sir John Norreys in the reign of Henry VI. There are eighteen shields, showing the arms of the founder of the house, his sovereign, patrons and friends—a *liber*

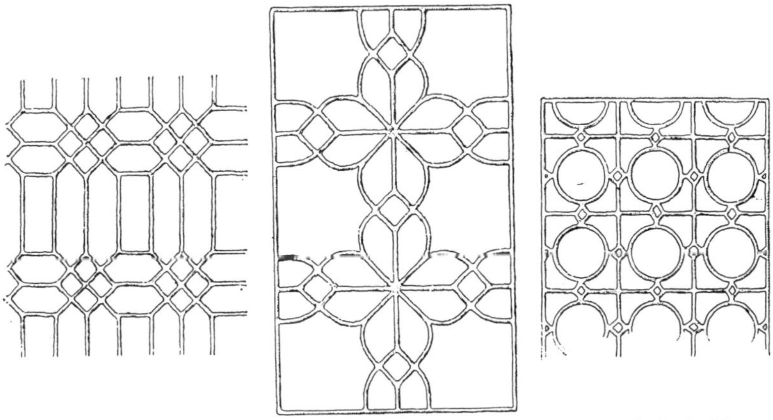

Broadway *Sherborne House* *Bramhall Hall*

PATTERNS OF LEAD GLAZING

amicorum—a not unpleasant way for light to come to us. As Mr. Everard Green happily says :[1] "Sir John Norreys believed that friendships were *duets in the psalm of life*, and by means of heraldry he recorded his friendships, thereby adding to the pleasures of memory as well as to the splendour of his great hall. His eye saw the shield, his memory supplied the story, and to him the lines of George Eliot,

> O Memories,
> O Past that IS,

were made possible by heraldry."

[1] *Archæologia*, Vol. 56, p. 324, where a full description of the shields will be found.

The common pattern of lead glazing was the diamond lattice-shaped pane, but there is an immense variety ; some are octagonal, or sexagonal with small diamond panes grouped around them, as in the example at Broadway. Walter Gedde published in 1613 *A Booke of Sundry Draughtes, Principally serving for Glaziers*, in which he gives over a hundred pages of designs. These are very complicated and intricate, and the Elizabethan or Jacobean glazier preferred simpler arrangements for his windows. Professor Lethaby in his book on *Leadwork* records some very intricate examples of lead glazing.

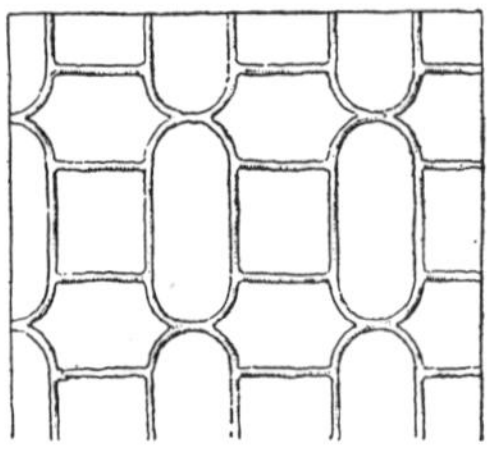

Sherborne House

PATTERN OF LEAD GLAZING

The diamond panes, or patterns based upon a variation of the diamond and square, seem to have been the earliest form of glazing. Occasionally when square panes are used the tops of the lights are rounded, so as to give a little artistic variety. Patterned leading sometimes fills the oval windows in the gables. Ventilating unglazed panes were introduced, filled with an open leadwork pattern. The glass that appears in old windows is remarkable. We like to have our windows filled with clear transparent glass. Our forefathers were content with a less perfect manufacture, and the colour of their glass varied from pale amber to bottle-green.

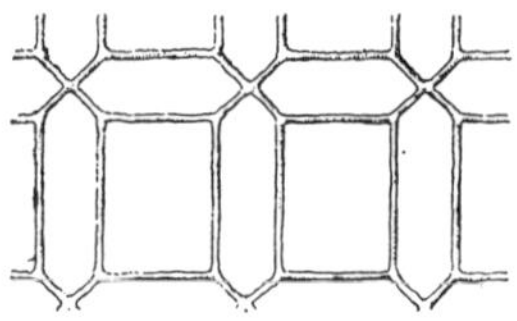

Owlpen

PATTERN OF LEAD GLAZING

Heraldic glass was fashionable in all Tudor houses, and the squire loved to see his coat-of-arms quartered with those of his wife in his windows, with his and her initials blended together, and sometimes, as at Ockwells, the arms of his friends also. If Queen Elizabeth in her many wanderings honoured him with a visit, the royal arms, the Tudor rose and E.R. would very shortly appear in stained glass or carved on panels or plastered on his ceilings. There were some noted artists in glass, such as the Dutchman Bernard Dininckhoff, who was working in England at the close of the sixteenth century, and Robert Wright, who made all the old glass at Hengrave Manor in 1567. An old account states that he was paid four pounds for the "making of all the glasse windows of the Manour-place, with the sodar, and for xiij skutchens with armes." A fine piece of armorial glass is illustrated from Franks House, presumably the work of an English hand.

LEADED PAINTED GLASS, FRANKS KENT, 1591

These windows with their "skutchens" impress upon the manor-house the stamp of ownership, the personality of the family. They light again the lamp of memory, recording the traditions, marriages and friendships of the owners, as do the carved arms and initials over the doorway. Too many of them are broken and gone like the family who once owned the manor; an additional reason for the careful guardianship of those still remaining.

VII

METAL-WORK

TUBAL CAIN, the first artificer in metals, has had many worthy followers in England who have added to the beauty of the manor-houses of this country. The local blacksmith was a cunning man who could work well and wonderfully, producing refined and highly decorated objects in iron, marvellously constructed framework for inn-signs, richly ornamented iron gates, as well as various beautiful things for the village church, and much else that we love to see to-day and fain would imitate.

LEADWORK

The ancient plumber or lead-worker adorned our country houses with many evidences of his skill. He has an ancestry of nearly two thousand years, and in his early days used to cover our houses, castles and churches with roofs of lead which were meant to last for ever. His art has fallen into desuetude, and cheap cast-iron stack-pipes, rain-water heads, cisterns and fountains have replaced the picturesque forms which delight us when we see them in old houses and gardens. We must look for some of the triumphs of his skill in the buildings of the sixteenth, seventeenth and eighteenth centuries. As early as the fourteenth century, so Viollet-le-Duc states, in England, and in no other country, lead pipes were used to convey the water from the roof to the base of the wall. These were usually square, and hence, he says, they could expand when the water froze, whereas a circular pipe could only burst. These pipes and heads and roofs were all made of cast lead, and not of milled or rolled

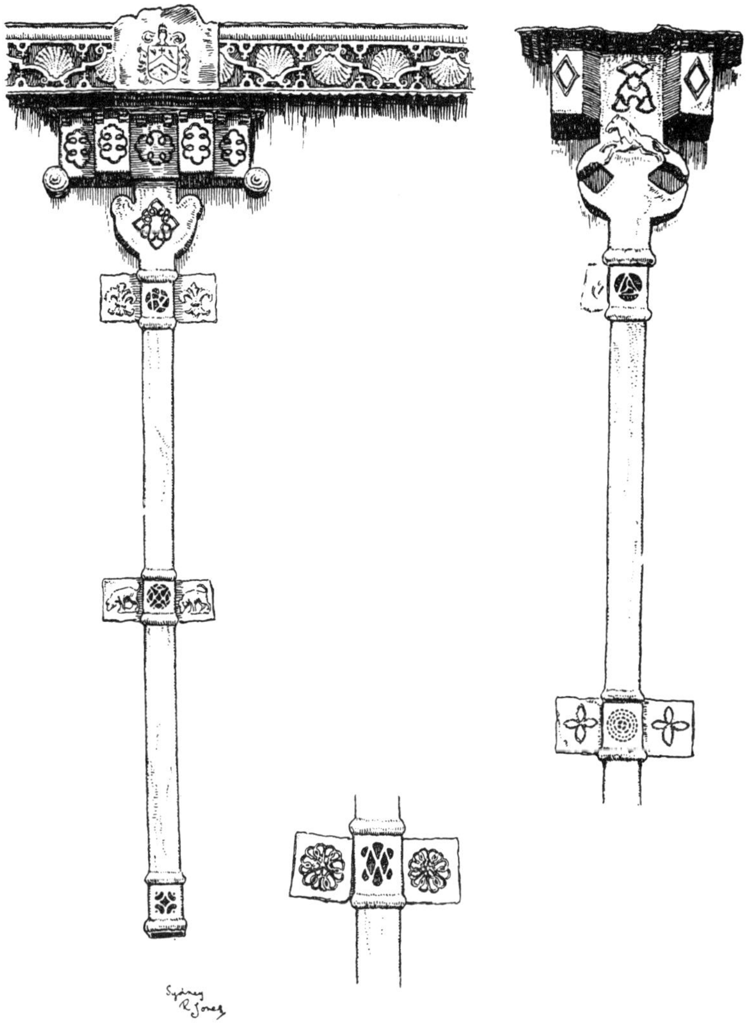

THREE EXAMPLES FROM WARWICKSHIRE

lead, a process which came into existence in the time of Wren, who did not favour it. The old lead was cast in sand, and this sand was naturally used for the impression of dates, letters and patterns which add beauty and interest to our old buildings.

OWLPEN MANOR

CANONS ASHBY
NORTHAMPTONSHIRE

The gutters of many old houses are adorned with little lead parapets, the front edge being cut into notches like that at Owlpen. Sometimes this decoration takes the form of small battlements, or has a pattern cast on it, or a scroll of flowery ornament.

Much ingenuity is displayed in the treatment of pipe-heads, which took the place of the mediæval gargoyle. The "lamp of memory" shed light on them, as on them were often represented the arms of the family or the initials of the builder, or the date when they were erected. Haddon Hall has a remarkable series of great variety of design and date. Professor Lethaby[1] writes :—

"The general form of these is constructed like a box from cast-sheet

[1] *Leadwork*, p. 140.

lead, the cornices are beaten to their shape over a pattern; and the top edge is cut into a little fringe of crenellations. Cast discs of ornament, badges, pendent knobs, and initials are arranged on their fronts, on the funnel-shaped portion leading to the pipe, and on the ears of the pipe, and the side flaps of the head itself. The more elaborate heads have an outer casing of lead with panels pierced through it of delicate tracery work of Gothic tradition which shows bright against the shadow."

HALL I' TH' WOOD

A very fine pipe-head appears at Canons Ashby, moulded and bent into a vase-like form and elaborately decorated with a leaf-shaped ornament and a human face. It bears the initials E. D., evidently an ancestor of Sir Alfred Dryden, the present owner. Quite as elaborate are the three examples taken from an old house in Warwickshire, which describe themselves. Notice the arms of the owner at the top; the elaborate shell and scroll pattern that runs along the gutter; the beautifully decorated lead bands that fasten the pipe to the wall, on the ends of which are stamped the *fleur-de-lis*, a hound and rosette. The horn and device above are probably a merchant's mark. We notice the curious way in which the band in the Canons Ashby example is bent back and curled like the scroll of a mediæval text.

PACKWOOD HOUSE

The pipe-head at Hall i' th' Wood, in Lancashire, is of simple design, dated 1648, with the initials A. N. A. It would have been well if the lead-worker had clung to this simplicity, and not wandered away in later times and tried to excel in producing *tours-de-force* of workmanship. The head and pipe at Packwood House, Warwickshire, form a charming model.

Lead was used for many other objects. Our ancestors were evidently not afraid of lead-poisoning, as they frequently made their cisterns of this substance, the sides of which they decorated with panels and ornaments, flowers and animals. We give an illustration of one that bears the date 1744, and

A LEAD CISTERN

is typical of the period. Pumps, too, were made of lead and adorned with arms and flowers and initials. In the garden we shall see some leaden statues and vases and urns, if the landscape gardener has left any of these relics when with ruthless hand he swept away the formal garden.

IRONWORK

Ironwork in England has had many vicissitudes. Its story would take too long to tell fully. The mediæval smith could fashion well and worthily. He made elaborate hinges, knockers, chests and grilles; rich scrollwork he hammered out, and in the thirteenth century used stamps and dies which could be impressed on hot iron, producing grand effects. Many fine railings for tombs were wrought by him, and doubtless he would have achieved many triumphs of artistic workmanship if wars and frequent disputes had not distracted him from his proper work, and turned his

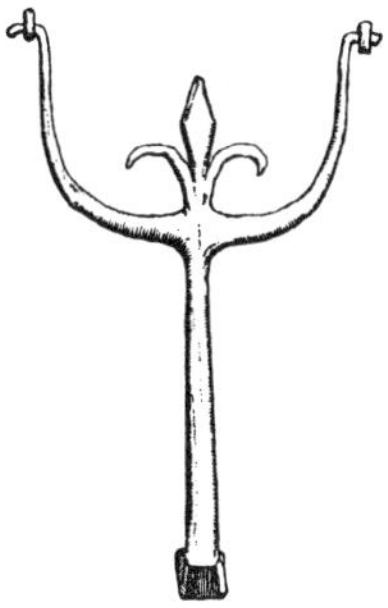

RUSHALL HALL
STAFFORDSHIRE

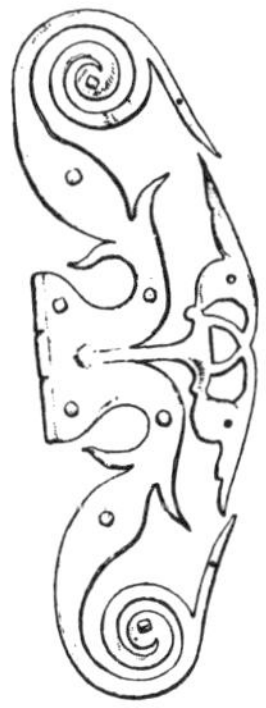

DITCHEAT PRIORY
SOMERSET

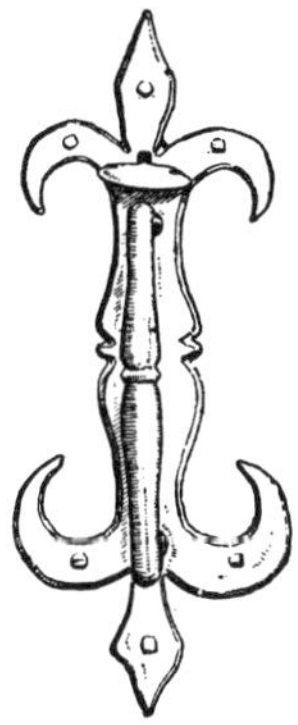

PACKWOOD HOUSE
WARWICKSHIRE

attention to the battlefield where his brawny arms were in much request as a fighter and a mender of weapons and armour. Hence true smithcraft languished, though it never

NUNUPTON COURT, HEREFORD

died out. No great revival took place in the Tudor and early Renaissance period. Henry VIII introduced foreign smiths into England, and sent ironfounders into Sussex,

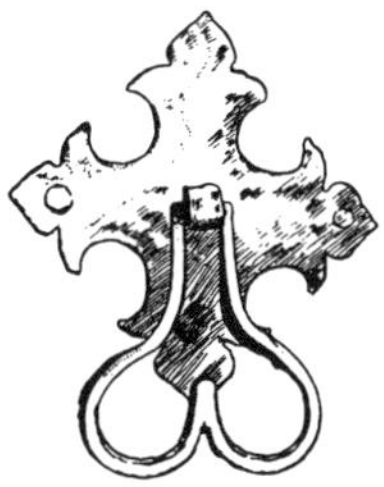

OWLPEN MANOR
GLOUCESTERSHIRE

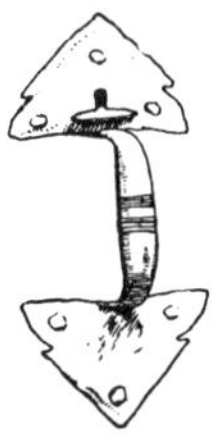

KINGSTON MANOR
ISLE OF WIGHT

OWLPEN MANOR
GLOUCESTERSHIRE

which then produced much of the metal of which the curious and elaborate firebacks were made. But genius showed itself in many villages where the smiths wrought cunningly such objects as the elaborate hinge at Ditcheat, or that at Nunupton Court, which might have been fashioned by a Gothic artist for a church door. He especially showed his cleverness and originality in designing knockers for the entrance doors. Rushall Hall, Staffordshire, furnishes a good example. The latch also gave him opportunity for good work, examples of which can be seen at Packwood House, Warwickshire, and at Kingston Manor in the Isle of Wight.

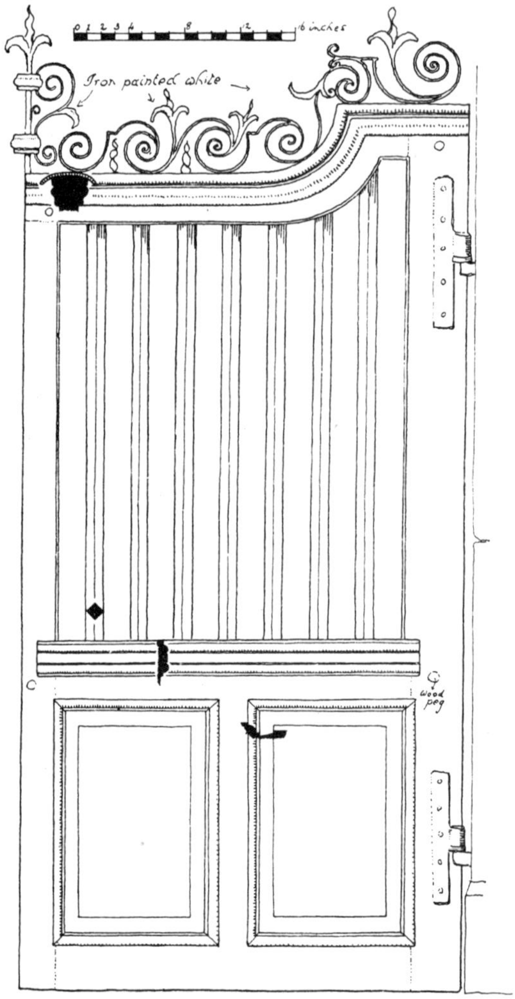

OWLPEN MANOR

Another example of good ironwork is shown at Owlpen; it is shaped like a shield with a row of *fleurs-de-lis* at the top. The background, which appears dark in the drawing, is of deep red velvet. There is, however, nothing very striking about these efforts, nothing that can rival the achievements of the carpenter and mason.

As regards gates, in the sixteenth and seventeenth centuries smithing had almost died out in England. Garden gates were constructed of wood, with, later, occasional bars of iron, and iron cresting. That at Owlpen is probably later than the gate itself. The curious gate at Packwood represents a style prevalent about latter part of the seventeenth century.

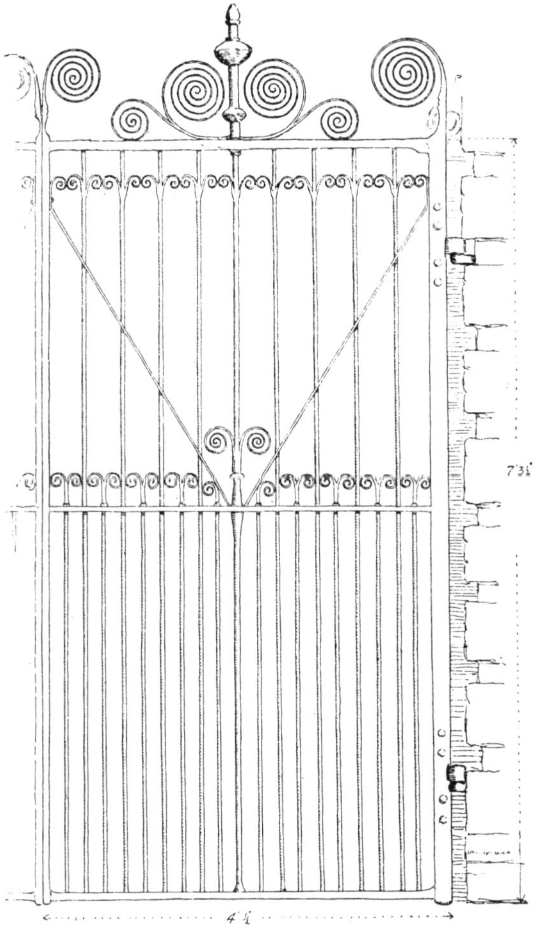

ONE OF A PAIR OF GATES TO THE FORE-COURT, PACKWOOD HOUSE, WARWICKSHIRE

Architects like Inigo Jones and his imitators cared nothing for smithcraft. Sir Christopher Wren did not encourage it, and it was not until the accession of William and Mary to the English throne, and the advent of one man, a famous and ingenious smith, that the art revived. This was Jean Tijou, a Frenchman, who had fled to Holland on the Revocation of the Edict

SANDYWELL, GLOUCESTERSHIRE

of Nantes in 1685, and came to England with "Dutch William." He did much work at Hampton Court, and

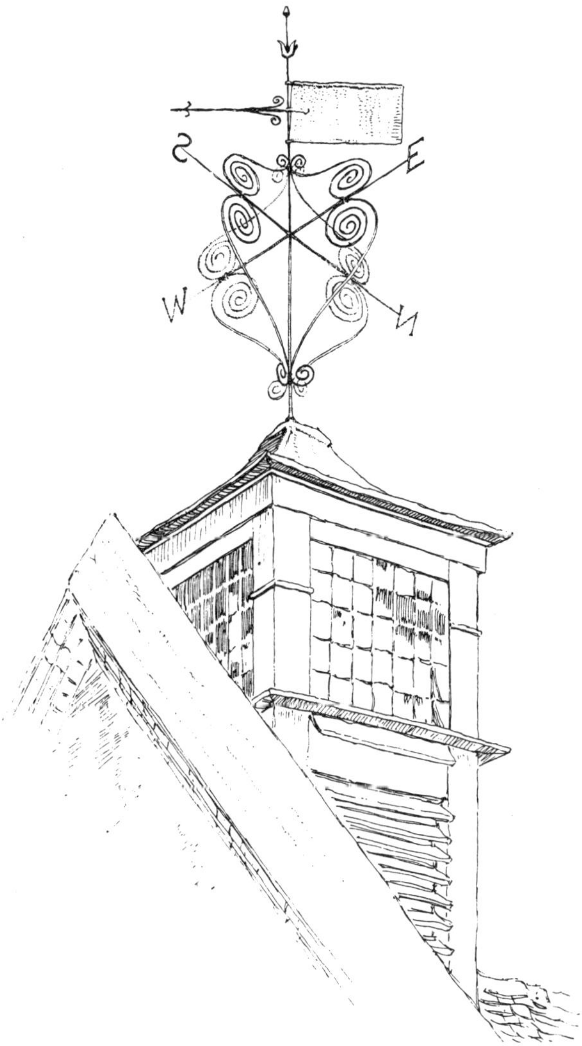

PACKWOOD HOUSE, WARWICKSHIRE

set an example which was followed by Thomas Robinson, the brothers Roberts, Bakewell, Warren, and others, who produced some of the finest pieces of ironwork in the country.

The elaborately constructed gates at Sandywell, Gloucestershire, are good examples of smithcraft, or the simpler specimen of those at Packwood, of which one gate is shown ; or the beautiful gates at the manor-house of Studley, Warwickshire (p. 38).

Another opportunity for smithcraft was found in the weathercocks, without which no manor-house was deemed complete. The vane usually appears on the stables or other out-building. It assumed divers shapes—an anchor, a horse, hound, ship, the crest of the family, and many other forms, and the shaft that supported it and held the iron rods pointing north, east, south and west, was decorated with much ingenious scrollwork and other adornments. The smith was very busy at Packwood, and probably fashioned the fine vane as well as the gates.

ST. MARY'S HOUSE, BRAMBER, SUSSEX

Some very curious and beautiful examples of smithcraft are found in St. Mary's House, Bramber, Sussex (see p. 81). That above is a window grille, and the work is probably of foreign origin. Indeed the various pieces of ironwork on the house would seem to have little connection with each other.

The many beautifully wrought window-fasteners to be found frequently in old houses present an unbroken tradition of fine smithcraft from mediæval days, till the sash window abolished the fitting. The most complete set which we have seen is in a house in the High Street of Guildford, and several old manor-houses retain these graceful examples of the smith's art.

But he fell on evil days. The brothers Adam and his followers designed their own decorations and cared naught for the craftsman, who languished and died out. During the early Victorian era his art was almost forgotten, and it was left to the men of the present generation, to Mr. J. Starkie Gardner and others, to revive the glories of their craft and make it again the means for the expression of true art.

VIII

GARDENS AND SURROUNDINGS

THE ideal manor-house is set in a framework that is worthy of it. It fits its site with due orderly accompaniment of garden and terraces. It was planned for use and comfort, but it never forgot to harmonize itself with its surroundings and to have a garden full of old-fashioned flowers, with clipped hedges and a paved or gravelled walk where the squire and his lady could take the air sheltered from cold winds. It is easier to discover a good manor-house garden than one attached to a more magnificent mansion. The country squire a century ago had the good taste not to follow the whims and fashions of his richer neighbours, nor to encourage the efforts of "Capability" Brown and other revolutionists to destroy the old pleasance and cultivate landscape gardening. This wild mania swept like a pestilence through the land, destroyed gardens wholesale, and "left the house a poor forlorn object set in a field of formless slopes and serpentine paths without relation to its surroundings."[1]

Perhaps a lighter purse preserved the squire from the enormities of his wealthier neighbours, but we will give him the credit of better taste and a true affection for the beauties of his old-fashioned garden.

In not a few cases, unfortunately, the garden has fallen on evil days. The bowling-green, where the old squire and his

[1] *English Houses and Gardens in the Seventeenth and Eighteenth Centuries*, by M. Macartney.

guests delighted to play a quiet game at bowls, and the lawn, once kept neat and trim, are a mass of rank grass. The fish-

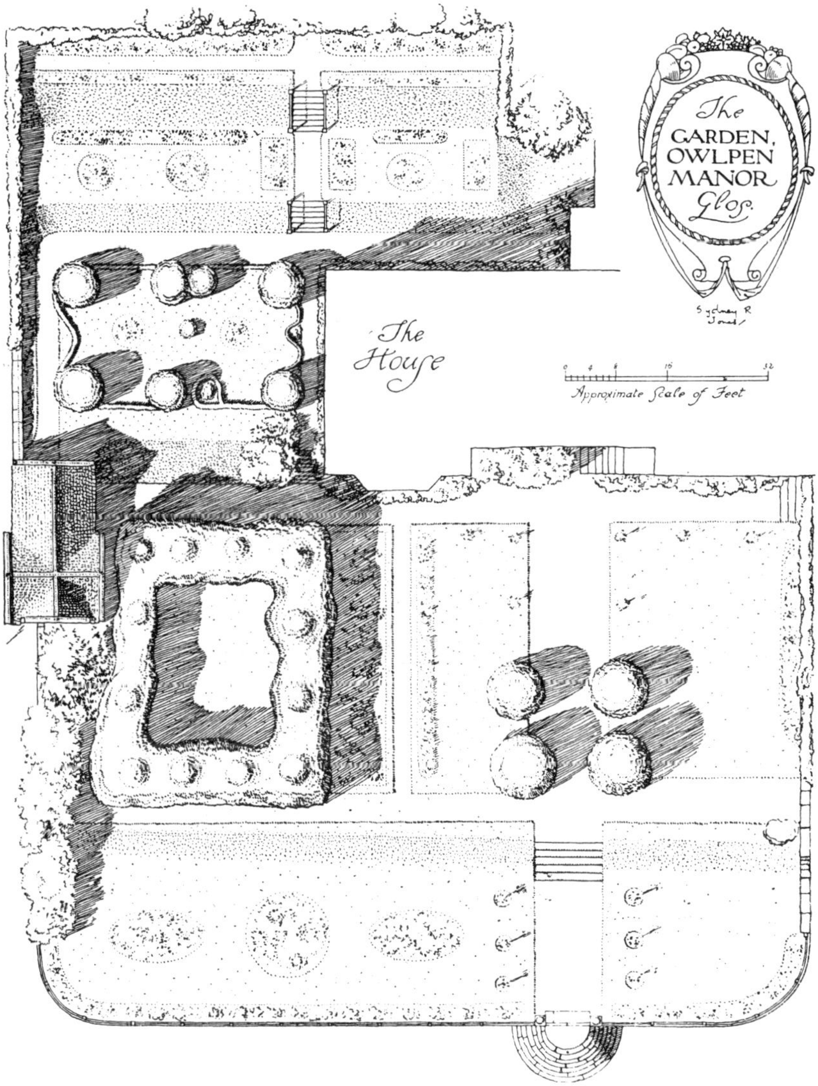

ponds are overgrown with weeds and rushes. Some of the old flowers struggle through crops of weeds. Hedges and shrubs have grown wild. Dead trees complete a scene of

CUT YEWS, OWLPEN MANOR, GLOUCESTERSHIRE

desolation which matches the fate of the family that has become extinct or has been compelled by poverty to let the house of their ancestors and live in retirement abroad, while the home becomes a farm and the garden is left to take care of itself. Happily all manor gardens are not like that.

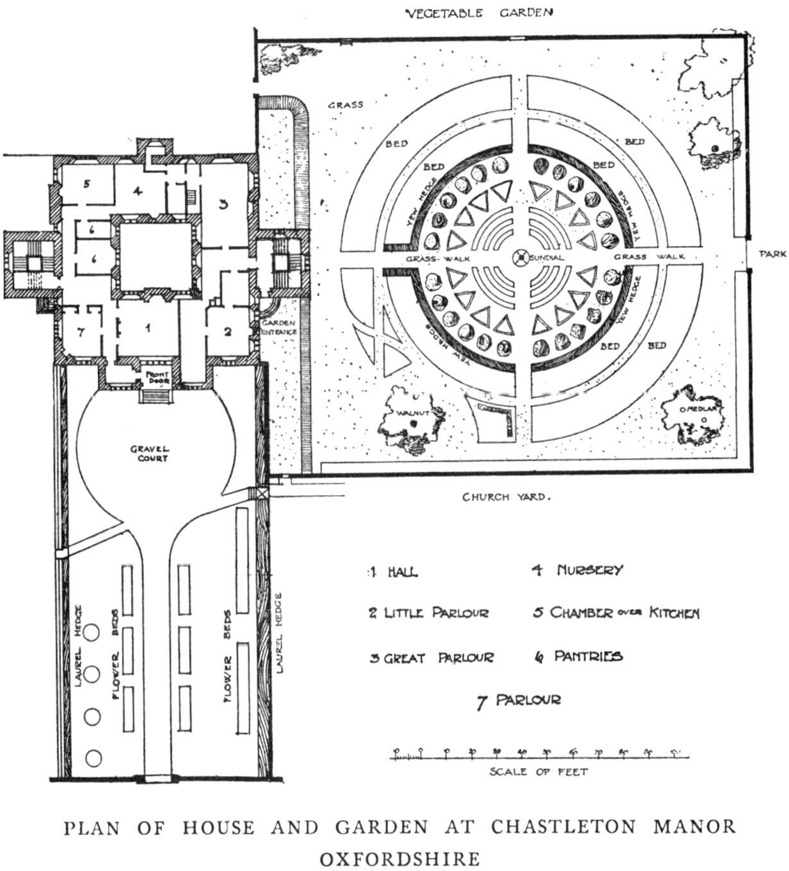

PLAN OF HOUSE AND GARDEN AT CHASTLETON MANOR OXFORDSHIRE

Owlpen Manor has a delightful garden which is typical of many others. Two views are shown of this. First there is the plan of the garden, and secondly the approach to the house along a sunken path with clipped yews on either side. The velvet lawns and parterres, the ingenious way in which

THE TERRACE GATEWAY AND STEPS, PACKWOOD HOUSE

the garden is divided and arranged, form fitting surroundings to this beautiful Tudor house.

The plan of the gardens at the typical Elizabethan manor-house of Chastleton (p. 191) is of much interest. A forecourt, which has a drive for carriages, gives access to the house, but the chief feature is the old circular garden to the east of the house. Inside the yew hedge is a ring of trees cut into numerous quaint animal and geometrical forms, many now scarcely to be distinguished.

Many manor-houses have avenues leading to them, such as West Court Manor, though it no longer leads to a drawbridge over a moat, as it once did. In some cases the avenues remain but the house has disappeared, destroyed during the Civil War of the seventeenth century. The great French gardener, Le Nôtre, who designed some of our English gardens, was devoted to avenues, the beauty of which we had, however, long realized before he influenced garden design. But these trees are outside the garden. Our forefathers loved arbours or bowers overspread with creepers, with vines and roses ; and in some few old gardens we find pergolas, which modern fashions have again decreed us to erect. They came to England with the Italian modes, and are named after a kind of grape which was trained over a trellis. We usually clothe our pergolas with crimson rambler. Parterres added diversity to the garden. These were of several kinds, the most common and beautiful being that formed of regular geometrically shaped beds with raised box edging, filled with flowers and separated from each other by little paths. There is a charming example of this at Warbrook, Eversley, a house built by John James, assistant architect to Sir Christopher Wren. Another form of parterre was constructed of grass plots cut into several pieces by intersecting paths. These were described in the old gardening books as *Parterres à l'Anglaise.*

Another charming feature of the old garden was the

THE ENTRANCE GATEWAY, EYAM HALL, DERBYSHIRE

terrace. In some cases where the slope of the ground was steep there were two or three terraces, as at St. Catherine's Court, Bath (p. 2). The hillside was cut away so as to form a level lawn with a level horizontal terrace walk above it. These terraces form agreeable shelters from the wind, and roses, shrubs and flowers thrive better than in any other part of the garden. Flights of steps lead up from the lower lawn to the upper terrace, along the edge of which runs a delightful balustrade, which acts as a parapet if the terrace is supported by a perpendicular wall. A pier stands on each side of the steps, sometimes supporting a fine iron gate, as at Packwood House. These gate-piers are usually square and plain, surmounted by an urn, or a stone ball, an obelisk, or the crest of the family.

The entrance gates to the garden may here be mentioned, of which we give several examples. The gateway at Eyam, Derbyshire, is imposing with its stone balls and imposts of great size, its posts quaintly decorated, its wooden gates of plain character and semicircular steps.

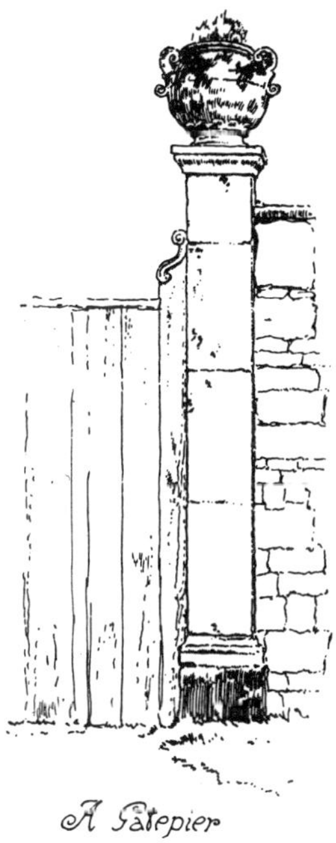

A GATEPIER AT CANONS ASHBY NORTHAMPTONSHIRE

We give an illustration of a gate-pier at Canons Ashby of plain character surmounted by an urn. Owlpen Manor has some attractive gates (pp. 54 and 182) which, except for the iron scrollwork at the top, are constructed of wood, the whole being painted white.

The garden was usually surrounded by a wall to guard its peace and preserve its seclusion. In this wall the builders often placed a doorway. There is a fine stone doorway in the wall of the garden at Winsley, Wilts, over which is placed an heraldic beast representing the crest of the family. It is dated 1657, but the door and opening have been renewed.

The topiary art was largely used in the old formal gardens and often carried to excess. A writer in the *Guardian*, September 29th, 1713, says :—

"How contrary to simplicity is the modern practice of gardening : we seem to make it our study to recede from nature, not only in the various tonsure of green into the most regular and formal shapes, but even in monstrous attempts beyond the reach of the art itself; we run into sculpture, and are yet better pleased to have our trees in the most awkward figures of men and animals than in the most regular of their own."

DOORWAY IN GARDEN WALL
WINSLEY, WILTSHIRE

It was an absurd fashion to hack trees into endless shapes, but a few carefully cut yews and box-trees in the form of peacocks are a comely feature of the formal garden, as in the beautiful new garden that Mr. E. Robinson Cox has caused to spring up around the grand old manor-house of South Wraxall in place of the old garden which time and neglect had almost obliterated.

Sometimes religious symbolism finds its expression in the number and arrangement of trees. Thus, at Cleeve Prior we find the twelve apostles and four evangelists typified in noble yew trees which are themselves symbolic of the

Resurrection. Fancy has woven an extraordinary conception in the beautiful gardens at Packwood, where we find the Sermon on the Mount set forth in clipped yew. There is a mount, a favourite feature in old gardens, and on its summit an arbour formed in a great yew tree, representing the Saviour ; four tall yews stand for the four evangelists, and six on each side for the twelve apostles, and leading up to these are "the multitudes," yews, box, Portugal laurels, which are supposed to be listening to the holy words of our Lord.

A SUNDIAL DATED 1660 AT PACKWOOD HOUSE

The garden at St. Catherine's Court, Somerset, illustrated on p. 2, shows a good example of clipped yews and a stone terrace, and the bird's-eye view of the garden at Chipping Campden shows the lay-out of the garden in relation to the house (p. 15).

No feature of an old garden is more charming than the sundial. We give some examples of these attractive details of garden architecture. They are of various forms and shapes, sometimes attached to a wall as at Marston Magna, Somerset, where the dial bears the motto, "As shadowe so man's life doth goe." A very picturesque dial is seen in the manor-house garden of Sutton Courtenay. Sometimes we have single figures supporting globes and spheres, and at Compton End, Winchester, there is a cross-dial mounted on a pedestal. The mottoes that sundials bear show much varying taste. There is usually a pathetic note struck, a *memento mori* sentiment. The following are some examples :—

> *Non numero horas nisi serenas.*
> *Carpe Diem.*
> *Suprema hæc multis forsan tibi.*
> *Festinat suprema.*
> *Nec momentum sine linea.*

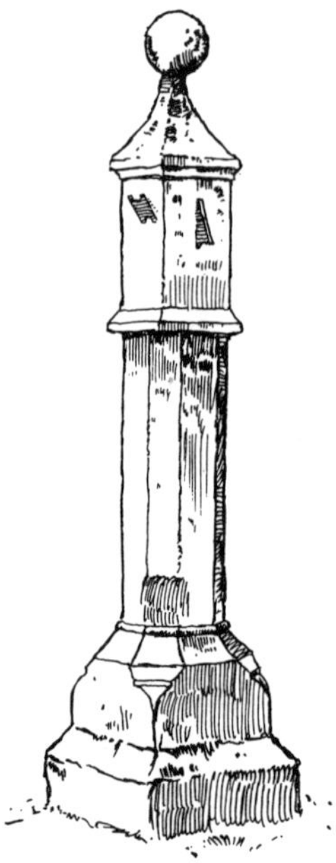

AT SUTTON COURTENAY

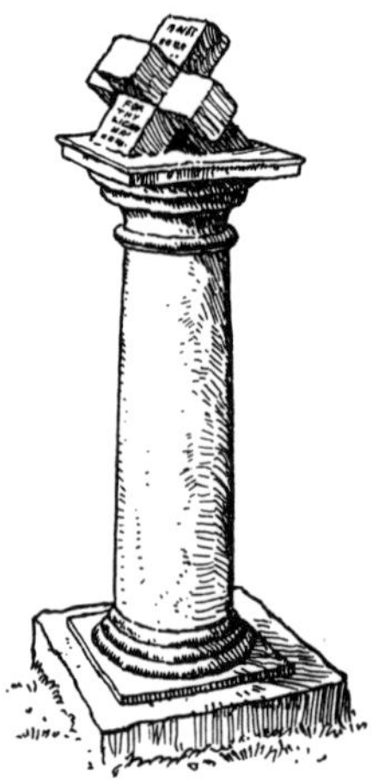

AT COMPTON END
WINCHESTER

It will be seen from these examples and from the other numerous mottoes inscribed on the mantelpieces, over the entrance door, along the panelling, that the old squire was very proud of his knowledge of Latin, and liked to adorn his house with many apt and profitable inscriptions. He loved his jokes, ingenious puns upon his name, as at Loseley House, near Guildford, where the gentleman, named More, who built the house made many rebus allusions to his name, representing a mulberry tree (*morus*) in one of his rooms, and round this *morus tardi moricus, morum cito moriturum.*

Pieces of water form a pleasing adjunct to a garden. Many manor-houses have preserved their moats, which add beauty now, where in former days they gave security. The illustration of Crowhurst (p. 27) shows this charming feature of an old manor-house. Fishponds are nearly always found in the grounds of an old house in order to provide fish for Lent and for Friday's dinner. Coarse fish are not appreciated by modern folk, and the fishpond has lost its utility; but it remains a thing of beauty, and when, as at Barkham Manor, water-lilies have been made to grow in it, and all kinds of lovely plants adorn its banks, and when rock-gardens are formed at its head, and a rustic bridge is made to cross it, it becomes a very charming feature. In some of the great gardens of mansions you find artificial canals, cascades and fountains, as at Chatsworth, the work of Grelly the French artist, but these schemes which entail a knowledge of engineering are too ambitious for the ordinary country squire.

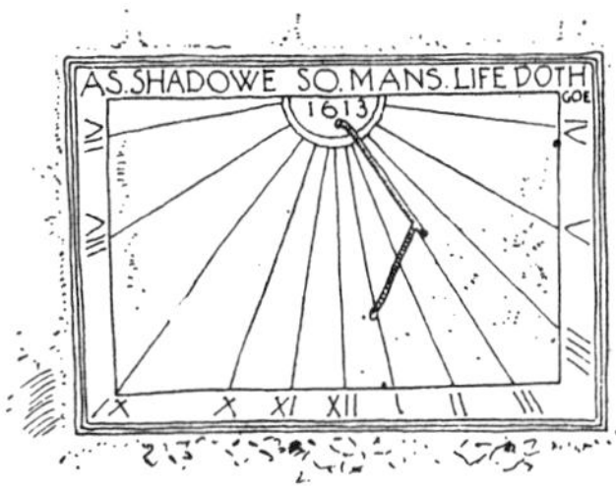

A WALL DIAL AT THE MANOR HOUSE, MARSTON MAGNA, SOMERSET

The formal garden often boasted of some statuary. In the pleasances of the great, during the prevalence of the Italian style, large stone or plaster statues of Roman soldiers in armour were frequently erected. At an earlier date, towards the end of the eighteenth century, leaden figures became fashionable, a fashion that is being revived. Professor Lethaby quotes Gray's letter, wherein the poet writes, "How charming it must be to walk in one's own garden, and sit on a bench in the open air with a fountain and a leaden statue and a rolling-stone and an arbour," and adds, "a statue that would be tame in stone, or contemptible in marble, may well be a charming decoration if only in lead, set in the vista of a green walk against a dark yew hedge or broad-leafed fig, or where the lilac waves its plumes above them, and the syringa thrusts its flowers under their arms and shakes its petals on the pedestal." A charming description truly! We give an illustration of a life-size figure of a shepherd playing a flute which appears in the garden of Canons Ashby. London gardens had many examples, and in our country gardens we find there attractive statues representing Father Time, flower girls, Hercules, Pan, negroes, Venus and "all heathen goddesses so fair," Mars, besides real heroes or illustrious personages. Sad has been their fate. They have been treated with great disrespect by their owners, and are getting very scarce. A very pleasing example has been recently introduced into the garden of South Wraxall Manor. Some others were recently sold at Christie's and realized large sums. The fortunate possessors of the once despised leaden statue will begin to prize their treasures and not part with them easily.

AT CANONS ASHBY

A feature of many an old house was the forecourt, of which Canons Ashby furnishes us with an example. In most instances it has disappeared. In large houses there were two or three of these courts. You could not drive in your coach up to the entrance door because a tiresome forecourt guarded by gates and paved with stone obliged you to get out of your coach and walk in the pouring rain to the door. Our forefathers being practical people, saw

AT CANONS ASHBY

this inconvenience, and the forecourt was doomed ; but in some old houses it still remains, as in the illustration of Canons Ashby.

We have described the manor-house garden, but we have not told of its wealth of flowers, its glorious roses of the old-fashioned sorts—Sweet Briar, Cabbage, York and Lancaster, Moss, old White Damask, the double white brother of pretty pink Maiden's Blush. The weather-toned brick walls look almost colourless by contrast with the rich crimson flowers of the Pyrus Japonica. That border on each side the central path of the walled garden with its fountain in the centre is gay with Sweet Williams, irises, peonies, pinks, carnations, wallflowers and Canterbury bells. It is a fair and beautiful place—this manor-house garden—and its sun-dial chants an endless song :—

Amydst ye flowres
I tell ye houres.
Tyme wanes awaye
As flowers decaye.
Beyond the tombe
Fresh fflowrets bloome,
Soe men shall ryse
Above ye skyes.

INDEX

Note.—The use of black *figures* denotes that the page reference is to an illustration.
A reference in the text will usually be found near an illustration, even when it has not been thought necessary to index it specifically.

A

Abel, John, architect of timber buildings, 70

Adam, The Brothers, 36, 172, 187

Aldermaston Manor, 14; newels at, 158

Angle-posts, carved, 68

Anne of Denmark, connection with Inigo Jones, 34

Appleton Manor, Berks, 18

Armorial Bearings, *see* Coats-of-arms

Atworth Manor-house, **128**; porch, 129

Avenues, 193

B

Bacon, Lord, on Renaissance rooms, 35; inveighs against large windows, 130

Ballingdon Old Hall, 112, 111; bay windows at, 131

Barge-boards, 24, **69**, 70, **134**; indicate age of building, 70, 136

Barkham Manor, fish-pond at, 199

Barnham Broom Old Hall, description of features, 92, 93; entrance door, 128, 126

Barningham Hall, four-storeyed porch at, 124

Barns, mediæval, 20; at Preston Bermondsey, 21

Batt, Henry, of Oakwell Hall, 52

Bay Windows, 31, 50, 76, 132, 57, **89**, 91, 111, 113

Berkshire, Appleton Manor-house, 18; Charney Bassett, 22; Ockwells Manor, 173; Steventon, 113

Bess of Hardwick, 130, 165

Boorde, Dr. Andrew, *Dyatary of Helth*, 32

Boothby Family, 18

Boothby Pagnell Manor-house, Norman, 18, 19; plan of, 31, 19

Bott's Green House, 8, 74, 7; features of, 8

Brackets, 24, 68, 84; from Tong, 69

Bradley Hall, 76, 77

Brereton, Uryan, of Handforth Hall, 78

Brick Chimneys from Norfolk, 117; from Warwickshire and Worcestershire, 119. (*See* also Chimneys)

Brick Details from East Kent, **98–9**

Brick Houses, 86-102, **87–104**

Brickmaking, 86

Brickwork, 36; in East Anglia, 90, 138; in Kent, 94

Bricks and Mortar, 88

Bridgnorth, gable at, 136, 69

Broad Street, Kent, 83; dormer at, 131; gable at, 84

Broadway, lead-glazing, 174, 173

BROCKHAMPTON HALL, *see* LOWER BROCKHAMPTON
BRONTË, CHARLOTTE, association with Oakwell Hall, 54
BROWNLOWE, LAURENCE, builder of Hall i' th' Wood, 80
BUCKINGHAMSHIRE, Newport Pagnell, 18; Penn, 131, 104
BUILDINGS, harmony of, with their surroundings, 40
BUR (West Bower Farm), 46-8, 47; supposed birthplace of Jane Seymour, 46; turrets with old glass, 46–8
BURFORD, battlemented chimneys at, 117
BURLINGHAM ST. EDMUND, three-storeyed porch at, 124

C

CALGARTH OLD HALL, mantelpiece at, 151
"CANE STONE," 40
CANONS ASHBY, forecourt, 201; gate-pier, 195; leaden statue, 200; pipe-head, 179, 178
"CAPABILITY" BROWN, 188
CARK HALL, Renaissance doorway at, 67; Tudor gabled house, 67, 43
CARTLEDGE HALL, 50–2, 52; ceiling, 166–7; clock case, 164; panelling, 161
CARVING, JACOBEAN, 163, 129. (*See* also references to Mantelpieces, Panelling, and Porches)
"CAUSEY" OF STEVENTON, 114
CAVENDISH HOUSE, 109; plastered timber, 112
CAVENDISH, SIR WILLIAM, of Hardwick, 165
CEILINGS, 165–72, 166–71; method of construction, 170; at Barnham Broom, 92; Hall i' th' Wood, 82
CHARNEY BASSET MANOR-HOUSE, 22; hall with wings, 22
CHASTLETON HOUSE, 30–1; plan of, with garden, 191; circular garden at, 193
CHESHIRE, Handforth Hall, 136, 79, 135
CHIMNEYPIECE, *see* MANTELPIECES
CHIMNEYS, 115–21, 116–21; fires in, 8; at Bradley, 76; Cark, 67; Preston, 22; Wilderhope, 56–8; from the Cotswolds, 116–17, 118; Kentish houses, 97; Warwickshire and Worcestershire, 119; St. Benedict's Priory, Kent, 121
CHIMNEY SHAFTS, 116
CHIMNEY-STACKS, beautifying of, 117–20; decline of importance, 121; elaboration, 117–20; at Harton Manor, 76; Nunupton Court, 99
CHIPPING CAMPDEN, 14; old view of, 15; chimneys at, 117, 118; garden at, 197
CISTERNS, LEAD, 180
CLARENDON PALACE, 18; spiral staircase at, 153
CLEEVE PRIOR, yews at, 196-7
CLOCK-CASE, at Cartledge, 164
COAT-OF-ARMS, on the chimneypiece, 146, 149; on the fireback, 152; on glass, 173, 175; on lead, 178; on the porch, 124, 122–4, 144
COMPTON END, sundial at, 197, 198
CONDOVER HALL, 58, 102
COOMBE SYDENHAM, Jacobean porch, 125, 122
COTSWOLD STONE, 134
COTSWOLDS, architectural character of the, 46; chimneys, 116, 118; dormers, 131; Whittington Court, 4, 5
COURT, quadrangular, rooms arranged round, 30, 33
COW-HAIR, use of, in construction of ceilings, 169-70
COXE, Judge, of Lower Lypiatt, 35
CRABBE, GEORGE, 90
CROMPTON, SAMUEL, at Hall i' th' Wood, 80

INDEX

CROWHURST PLACE, 26, 27; moat at, 199
CROWN HOUSE, NEWPORT, 107; external pargework at, 109; shell porch at, 108
CROW-STEPPED GABLES, 88, 92, 94, 93, 132
CUPBOARD DOORS, 65-6, 164, 163
CUP-DOG, 153, 150
CURVED BRACES, 136, 69; at Harton, 76, 75
CURVED GABLES, 94, 138, 97, 101, 103

D

DAUNT, JOHN, of Owlpen, 54
DE STANTON FAMILY, 48
DENHAM, SIR JOHN, 58
DERBYSHIRE, Eyam Hall, 195, 66; Haddon Hall, 178; Melbourne Hall, 159; Padley Hall, 20; Stanton Old Hall, 117, 49, 143
DESTRUCTION OF OLD HOUSES, 8
DEVONSHIRE, West Down Manor-house, 151; Potheridge House, 171
DINGLEY, JOHN, of Wolverton, 62; Sir John, 64
DININCKHOFF, BERNARD, artist in glass, 175
"DINING PARLOUR," 33
DITCHEAT PRIORY, 28, 29; buttery hatches and screen, 141; hinge, 182, 181
DOG-GATES, 52
DOOR, at Barnham Broom, 128, 126; Hall i' th' Wood, 82
DOOR-HEAD (stone), at Wormleighton, 124
DOORWAY (garden), at Winsley, 195, 196
DOORWAYS, *see* PORCHES
DORMERS, 131; at Broad Street, 83; Kirstead, 95; Nunupton, 102; Penn, 104
DORSET, Sandford Orcas, 51, 116
DOVECOTS, at Parham Old Hall, 90; Shipton Hall, 56
DRIPSTONES, 50, 58, 125

E

E-SHAPED HOUSE, 33, 62
EAST BARSHAM, 90; decorated chimney-stack at, 118–20
EAST HENDRED, five manors of, 14
ELIZABETHAN HOUSE, the, 33
ELSING HALL, 106; chimney, 118
ESCOTE GREEN, chimney-stack at, 120, 119
ESSEX, Ballingdon Old Hall, 131, 111; Crown House, Newport, 110, 129, 107, 108; Falkbourn Hall, 88; Loughton Hall, 153; Saffron Walden, 112; Sandon Manor-house, 18; Wyvenhoe, 112
EVESHAM, a barge-board from, 70
EYAM HALL, 66; history of, 67; entrance gate at, 195, 194

F

FASCIA BOARD, 69
FINCHAMPSTEAD, two manors at, 14
FINIALS, 137-8; at Kingston, I.O.W., 137; Merstone, 137; Moor Hall, 137; Owlpen, 137; Whittington, 138
FIRE-BACKS, 153, 151-2
FIRE-DOGS, 153, 150
FIRES IN CHIMNEYS, 8
FIREPLACES, 18; at South Wraxall, 60-2. (*See* MANTELPIECES)
FISH-PONDS, 199
FLEMINGS, THE, in Eastern England, 70; re-introduction of brick by, 86, 88
FLINT HOUSES, 104, 105
FLINT IN CHALK DISTRICTS, 104
FLINTWORK WITH BRICK OR STONE, 104-6, 105
FORECOURTS, 200-1; at Canons Ashby, 200, 201; Chastleton, 193; Wolverton, 62
FRANKS HOUSE, armorial glass at, 175

G

GABLES, 70, 135-9, 132-7; crow-stepped, 88, 93, 95, 132; curved,

94, 101, 103; in East Kent, 98–9; foreign influence on, 94, 138; seventeenth-century, 94; at Bradley Hall, 77; Bridgnorth, 136, 69; Broad Street, 83; Littlebourn, 94, 97–9; Sarre, 44

Gallery, feature of Elizabethan house, 33; at Oakwell Hall, 52

Gallery, Minstrel, 22

Gardens, 188–202; cut yews at Owlpen, 190; forecourts, 200, 201; gateways, 195, 192, 194; pergolas in, 193; plan of, at S. Catherine's Court, 1; at Chastleton, 191; at Owlpen, 189; sundials, 197–9; terraces, 195–7, 15; gateways, 195, 192, 194; gateway at Eyam, 194

Gatehouse, at Sandford Orcas, 50, 51

Gatehouses, Timber, 24, 25; Tudor, 51

Gate-piers, at Atworth, 128; Canons Ashby, 195; Owlpen, 55; Packwood, 195; Studley, 38; Wooton Wawen, 127

Gates, 183–6; to gardens, 195; at Lower Lypiatt, 35, 37; Studley, 38

Gateway, *see* Gates, etc.

Glass, heraldic, at Franks House, 173, 175; leaded, 173

Gloucestershire, Campden House, 14, 15; Lower Lypiatt, 37; Moor Hall, 138; Owlpen, 54, 55, 137, 162, 178, 182, 190; Sandywell, 184; Wanswell Court plan, 32; Warren House, 168; Whittington Court, 4, 58, 5, 118, 138, 142, 146–7, 156

Great Chalfield, ancient glass, 172–3; masks, 60; moat, 28; plan, 31, 34

Great Chamber, The, 158

Great Lyth, The, 101–2, 103

Great Snoring, 90; chimney, 118

Great Tangley, Surrey, 26, 82

Grimshaw Hall, timber and plaster house, 75, frontispiece

Groby Old Hall, 98, 100; historical interest, 99

Gunpowder Plot Conspirators, 72–4

Gutters, with lead parapets, at Owlpen, 178

Gwyn, Nell, association with Crown House, Newport, 110

H

H-shaped House, 33

Haddon Hall, pipe-heads at, 178

Half-timber, *see* under Timber

Hall, chief apartment of old houses, 17, 24, 31; disuse of, 33; at Charney Basset, 22; Lower Brockhampton, 22, 23

Hall i' th' Wood, 78–82, 80; panelling, 163, 161; pipe-head, 179; staircase, 158, 155

Hampshire, Warbrook, Eversley, 193; Warneford plan, 32

Handforth Hall, 76–8, 79; carving round door frame, 129; gable of, 136, 135

Hardwick, mantelpiece at, 150

Harringworth, chimney at, 116

Harton Manor-house, 76, 75

Harvington Hall, newels at, 158, 154

Heasley Manor, I.O.W., chimney-stack, 120

Hengrave Manor, old glass at, 175

Heraldic Decorations, *see* Coat-of-arms

Herefordshire, Lower Brockhampton, 23, 25, 134; Nunupton Court, 131, 101–2, 182; timber houses in, 72

Hidcote, chimneys at, 117, 118

Hinges, 182, 181

INDEX

HONFORDS OF HONFORD, 76–8
HORSHAM STONE, 134
HUDDINGTON COURT, Worcestershire, 72–4, 71; chimney-stack at, 120, 119; window-bracket, 131

I

INTERIOR DETAILS, 145–175, 146–175
INTERIORS, 141–5, 140–5
IRONSTONE, in Northamptonshire, 126
IRONWORK, 180–7, 181–6; decline of, 187; fittings, 182, 186; gates, 183–6; weathercocks, 186

J

JACOBEAN HOUSE, THE, 34
JONES, INIGO; ceilings of, 170; disuse of common hall in time of, 26; Palladian adaptations by, 34–5; porches of, 129; Raynham Hall by, 144, 140
JONES, JOHN, of Chastleton, 30

K

KENSWORTH MANOR, early Norman house, 18
KENT, brick and flint work in, 94; Broad Street, 131, 83; Franks House, 175; Littlebourne, 97, 98–9; The Old House, Sandwich, 169; Penshurst, 154; St. Benedict's Priory, 84, 41; Sarre, 94, 44, 98; Sturry Court, 96
KINGSTON MANOR, Isle of Wight, 64–6, 64; cupboard door at, 163; finial at, 137; kitchen at, 145; latch at, 181
KIRSTEAD OLD HALL, 92–4, 95; dormers, 131; three-storeyed porch, 124
KITCHENS, 18, 31; at Kingston, 65, 145
KNEELERS, 137–8, 135–6
KNILL COURT, timber house, 72
KNOCKERS, 181–2, 181; at Rushall, 182, 181; Owlpen, 181
KNOLE, fine mantelpiece at, 147
KNOOK MANOR, 60, 61

L

LANCASHIRE, Cark Hall, 67, 43; Hall i' th' Wood, 78–82, 80, 155, 161, 179
LANDSCAPE GARDENING, 188
LATCHES, 182, 181
LATHS, thickness of, in early work, 169
LAWKLAND HALL, 8, 9
LE NÔTRE, French gardener, 193
LEAD-GLAZING, 172–5; patterns of, 83, 173, 174
LEADED PAINTED GLASS, at Franks House, 175
LEADWORK, 176–80, 177–80; cisterns, 180; gutters, 178; pipeheads, 178–9; pipes, 177
LEICESTERSHIRE, Groby Old Hall, 98, 100
LETHABY, PROFESSOR, on leadwork, 199; on pargeting, 106–7
LINCOLNSHIRE, Boothby Pagnell, 31, 19
LINENFOLD PATTERN, 126; history of, 162–3
LITTLEBOURNE, 97; gables at, 94–6; brick details from, 98, 99
LITTLE WENHAM HALL, 86–8, 154, 87
LONG, Robert, of South Wraxall, 60; Sir Thomas Long, 60
LONGLEAT, 30; plaster-work at, 165
LORD OF THE MANOR, importance of the, 12
LOSELEY PARK, MS. at, 130; mantelpieces at, 147
LOUGHTON HALL, fireback at, 153, 151
LOWER BROCKHAMPTON HALL, gable of, 136, 134; gatehouse of, 24, 25; hall of, 22, 23
LOWER LYPIATT HOUSE, 35–6, 37

M

"Magpie" Houses, 78
Manor, The, definition of, 14; division of, 14; plan of, 13; story of, 11–14
Manor-house, The, barns of, 18–19; details of—exterior, 115–39; interior, 141–75; evolution of, 17–39; fourteenth-century, 24; fifteenth-century, description of typical, 24–5; Jacobean, 34; Norman, 17–18; quadrangular form of early, 18; "Queen Anne," 36; Saxon, 17; situation of, 14; Tudor, 28–34
Mantelpieces, 145–53, 140, 146–9; at Hall i' th' Wood, 82; Huddington Court, 74
Marston Magna, sundial at, 197, 199
Masks, Curious, at Great Chalfield, 60
Materials of Construction, 40–5. (*See* also under separate names, as Stone, Brick, Timber, etc.)
Melbourne Hall, eighteenth-century staircase, 160, 159
Merstone, kneeler at, 135
Metal-work, 153, 176–87, 150–1, 177–86
Meux Family, 65
Minstrel Gallery, 22
Moats, at Boothby Pagnell, 18; Crowhurst, 199, 27; Great Chalfield, 28; Huddington Court, 71; Lower Brockhampton, 24; Parham, 91; Ram Hall, 66; Wolverton, 62
Moor Hall, finial at, 137
Moreton Pinkney, kneeler at, 137
Mottoes on mantelpieces, 151; on sundials, 198, 202
Moulding, lapel, at Kingston, 65
Mouldings, brick and plaster, 92
Mullioned Windows, 130; at Broad Street, Kent, 83; Kirstead Old Hall, 95; Oakwell Hall, 53; Ram Hall, 65; Shipton Hall, 57

N

Newels, of stone (central), 153–6; of wood, 156–8, 154–9
Nonsuch Palace, plaster-work at, 165
Norfolk, brickwork in, 86, 90, 138; brick porches in, 124; Barnham Broom, 93, 126; Elsing Hall, 106, 118; Kirstead Old Hall, 92, 124, 131, 95; Raynham Hall, 144, 170, 140
Norman Houses, 17–18, 19
Norreys, Sir John, of Ockwells Manor, 173
Northamptonshire, Sulgrave, 125; Canons Ashby, 179, 195, 200, 201
Nunupton Court, decayed condition of, 99; chimney-stack at, 99; gables at, 99; timber porch at, 99, 101, 102; dormers at, 131; elaborate hinge at, 182, 181

O

Oak, *see* general references under Timber and Wood
Oakwell Hall, Birstall, 52–4, 53
Ockwells Manor, windows at, 173
Old Shoyswell, tile-hung, half-timbered house, 84–6, 85
Oriel Windows, frontispiece, 41, 83; at Solihull, 75, 73; in gateway at South Wraxall, 60
Owlpen Manor, 54, 55; gable at, 137; garden, plan of, 189; gate to garden, 195, 182; knocker, 181; lead gutter, 178; yews, 190
Oxfordshire, Coggs Manor-house, 22; Cottisford, 22; Broughton Castle, 164

P

Packwood House, clipped yews at, 197; garden gateway and steps, 192; gates, 183, 192;

INDEX

latch, 181; pipe-head, 179; sundial, 197; vane, 185
PADLEY HALL, 20
PANELLING, 160–5, 157, 161–4, 166
PARGETING (Parge-work), exterior plaster, 106-14, 107–13
PARHAM OLD HALL, 90–2, 91
PARTERRES, 193, 191
PAYNELL FAMILY, 18
PENN MANOR-HOUSE, 102, 104; dormers at, 131
PERGOLAS, 193
PIPE-HEADS, 177–9, 177–9; arms or initials on, 178
PITCHFORD HALL, half-timber house, 75, 102
PLASTERED BRICK, 92, 95
PLASTER MANTELS, 151-2, 149
PLASTER-WORK, 106–12, 151–2, 165–72
PORCHES, 121–9, 122–7; foreign influence on, 126-7; at Barnham Broom, 93; Bradley Hall, 77; Kirstead, 95; Nunupton, 102; Stockton, 105; Shell Porches, 129, 127; at Crown House, Newport, 108
POTHERIDGE HOUSE, DEVON, ceiling at, 170, 171
PRESTON BERMONDSEY (or Plucknett), 20, 21; barn, 22; octagonal chimney, 22
PRIESTS' HOLES, 76
PUMPS (lead), 180

Q

"QUEEN ANNE" HOUSES, 35–6, 37, 104

R

RAINWATER-HEADS, *see* PIPE-HEADS, 176–80
RAM HALL, 66, 65; moat and barn at, 66
RAYNHAM HALL, ceiling at, 170; Renaissance interior at, 144, 140
ROOFS, 132–5; construction of, 133; covered with stone slabs, 50, 134, 49, 51; with tiles, 133; hipped, 133–4, 104; signs of period, 133
RUSHALL HALL, door-knocker at, 182, 181
RUSKIN, 4–6

S

SAFFRON WALDEN, plaster-work on house at, 112
ST. BENEDICT'S PRIORY, Kent, 84, 41; chimney-stack at, 121
ST. CATHERINE'S COURT, 2; terrace gardens at, 195, 197
"ST. MARY'S," BRAMBER, 82–4, 81; window grille at, 186
SANDFORD ORCAS MANOR-HOUSE, 50; Tudor gatehouse at, 51; chimney-stacks at, 117, 11
SANDON MANOR-HOUSE, 18
SANDWICH, ceiling of The Old House, 170, 169
SANDYWELL, gates at, 186, 184
SARRE, brick and flint gable at, 94, 44; brick details from, 98
SAXON HOUSES, 17
"SCREENS," the, 26
SHELDON HALL, mantel at, 148; newels, 154; panelling, 162; staircase, 157
SHELL PORCH, the, 129; at Crown House, Newport, 110, 108; Wooton Wawen, 129, 127
SHIPTON HALL, Shropshire, 56, 57; bay windows at, 131
SHOYSWELL FAMILY, 85–6
,, HOUSE, *see* OLD SHOYSWELL
SHROPSHIRE, timber houses of, 75–6; variety of materials, 102; bracket at Tong, 69; Condover Hall, 58, 102; Great Lyth, 76, 103; Harton Manor-house, 75; Pitchford Hall, 75, 102; Shipton Hall, 131, 57; Wilderhope Manor, 59; Wyle Cop, 75
"SKUTCHENS," 175
SMALLMAN FAMILY, 56

SMITHCRAFT, decay and revival of, 183-4
SOLARS, 18; fireplaces first in, 115
SOLIHULL MANOR-HOUSE, 74-5, 73
SOMERSET, Coombe Sydenham, 122; Marston Magna, 199; Preston Bermondsey, 21; St. Catherine's Court, 195-7, 2; West Bower Farm, 47
SOUTH WRAXALL MANOR, 60; mantelpiece, 150
SPARROW'S HOUSE, Ipswich, plaster-work at, 112
SPENCER FAMILY, 89
SQUIRE, mediæval house of a, 24, 26
STAFFORDSHIRE, Bradley Hall, 77; Rushall Hall, 181
STAIRCASES, 153-60, 154-9; carving of, 158; construction of, 156-60; eighteenth-century, 160, 159; Jacobean, 158, 157; mediæval circular, 153-4; newels of, 153-8; steps of, 160
STANTON OLD HALL, 48, 49; plain interior of, 144, 143
STATUES, leaden, 200
STEVENTON, half-timbered buildings at, 112; plaster house at, 114, 113
STOCKTON MANOR, stone and flint house, 106, 105
STONE HOUSES, 46-67; districts famous for, 46
STONE-SLAB ROOFING, in Derbyshire, 50, 51; in Sussex, 134
STUDLEY MANOR-HOUSE, 36, 38; iron gates at, 186, 38
STURRY COURT, 94, 96
SUFFOLK, Cavendish Manor, 109; Little Wenham Hall, 86-8, 154, 87; Parham Old Hall, 90, 92, 91; Sparrow's House, Ipswich, 112
SULGRAVE, porch with sundial, 125
SUNDIALS, 197-8, 202, 197-9; mottoes on, 197-8, 202; variety of form of, 197; at Hall i' th' Wood, 80; over door at Sulgrave, 125
SUSSEX, Old Shoyswell, 84, 85; St. Mary's, Bramber, 82, 81, 186; Shrub Place, 42; Warnham Court, 150
SUTTON COURTENAY, three manors, 14; sundial at, 197, 198

T

TEMPLE, SIR WILLIAM, 3
TERRACES, 195, 2
THORPE, JOHN, architect, 34, 156
TIJOU, JEAN, master of smithcraft, 183, 186
TILE-HANGING, on walls, 84, 133, 85; patterns of, 133
TILE-ROOFING, 133-4
TIMBER GABLES, 70, 135-6, 69, 135
TIMBER HOUSES, 68-86, 25-7, 71-83; in the forest districts, 68; in Herefordshire, 72; in Shropshire, 75; signs of period of, 68-70
TOPIARY ART, 196
TUDOR HOUSES, 28-34, 5, 49, 51; building of, 30; porch important feature of, 124

V

VANES, 186; at Packwood, 185

W

WALLS, flint, with brick or stone, 104-5; tiled, 84, 133
WANSWELL COURT, 31; plan of, 32
WARNEFORD MANOR-HOUSE, 31; plan of, 32
WARNHAM COURT, fire-dogs and toasting-fork at, 153, 150
WARREN HOUSE, Stanton, ceiling at, 170, 168
WARREN, smith, 35, 36
WARWICKSHIRE, Bott's Green House, 8, 74, 7; Grimshaw Hall, 75, frontispiece; Packwood

House, 179, 181, 183, 185, 192, 197; Ram Hall, 65; Sheldon Hall, 148, 154-7, 162; Solihull, 73; Studley, 36, 186, 38; Wormleighton Manor, 89, 123
WATTLE AND DAUB, use of, for Saxon houses, 68
WEST BOWER MANOR, now Farm, *see* BUR
WEST DOWN MANOR, plaster mantels, 151
WESTMORLAND, Calgarth Old Hall, 151
WESTWOOD PARK, Worcestershire, 170
WHITTINGTON COURT, 4, 5; history of, 58-9; chimneys, 118; entrance hall, 142; finial, 138; mantelpieces, 146-7; newels, 156
WILDERHOPE MANOR, 56-8, 59
WILLIAMS, CHARLES, artist in plaster, 165
WILTSHIRE, Atworth Manor, 128; Great Chalfield, 28, 60, 172, 34; Knook, 61; Longford Castle, 106; Longleat, 165; South Wraxall, 60, 147, 196; Stockton Manor, 105
WINDOW-BRACKETS, 131; at Huddington, 131
WINDOW-FASTENERS, 186; in a Guildford house, 187
WINDOW-FRAMES, 132, 122, 132
WINDOW-GRILLE, at "St. Mary's," Bramber, 186
WINDOWS, 129-32, 132; bay, 131; frontispiece, 5, 41, 47, 91, 109, 111, 113; dormer, 131, 83, 104; in Cotswolds, 130-1; in East Anglia, 131, 132; oriel, 131; frontispiece, 41. (*See* also MULLIONED WINDOWS)
WINSLEY, doorway in garden wall, 195, 196
WOLVERTON MANOR, 62-4, 63; kneeler at, 136; porch of, 125
WOOTON WAWEN, shell porch at, 129, 127
WORCESTERSHIRE, Harvington Hall, 154; Huddington Court, 120, 131, 72, 119; Westwood Park, 170
WORMLEIGHTON MANOR, 89, 125, 89, 123-4; clock-tower, 123; door-head, 124; porch, 123
WREN, SIR CHRISTOPHER, 35; chimneys of, 121; plaster-work in time of, 170-1; porches of, 129
WRIGHT FAMILY, 67
WRIGHT, ROBERT, artist in glass, 175

Y

YEWS, CLIPPED, 196-7, 190
YORKSHIRE, Cartledge Hall, 50, 144, 52, 161, 164, 166-7; Lawkland Hall, 8, 9; Oakwell Hall, 53